Controversial Issues in Energy Policy

CONTROVERSIAL ISSUES IN PUBLIC POLICY

Series Editors
Dennis Palumbo and Rita Mae Kelly
Arizona State University

Controversial Issues in Energy Policy

Alfred A. Marcus

Controversial Issues in Public Policy
Volume 2

SAGE Publications
International Educational and Professional Publisher
Newbury Park London New Delhi

For information address:

SAGE Publications, Inc.
2455 Teller Road
Newbury Park, California 91320

SAGE Publications Ltd.
6 Bonhill Street
London EC2A 4PU
United Kingdom

SAGE Publications India Pvt. Ltd.
M-32 Market
Greater Kailash I
New Delhi 110 048 India

Printed in the United States of America

Library of Congress Cataloging-in-Publication Data

Marcus, Alfred Allen, 1950-
Controversial issues in energy policy / Alfred A. Marcus.
p. cm.—(Controversial issues in public policy; v. 2)
Includes bibliographical references and index.
ISBN 0-8039-3969-8 (cloth).—ISBN 0-8039-3970-1 (pbk.)
1. Energy policy. 2. Power resources. I. Title. II. Series.
HD9502.A2M348 1992
333.79—dc20 92-30003
CIP

92 93 94 95 10 9 8 7 6 5 4 3 2 1

Sage Production Editor: Judith L. Hunter

Contents

To the memory of my father, James Marcus, 1912-1992,
who understood the value of scarce resources.

Series Editors' Introduction

Public policy controversies escalated during the 1980s and early 1990s. This was partly due to bitter partisan debate between Republicans and Democrats, a "divided" government in which the Republicans controlled the presidency and the Democrats controlled the Congress, and the rise of "negative" campaigning in the 1988 presidential election. In addition, highly controversial issues such as abortion, crime, environmental pollution, affirmative action, and choice in education became prominent on the public policy agenda in the 1980s.

Policy issues in this atmosphere tend to be framed in dichotomous, either-or terms. Abortion is depicted as murder on the one hand and a woman's self-interested choice on the other. One is either tough on crime or too much in favor of defendants' rights. Affirmative action is a matter of quotas or a special interest issue. School choice is the means for correcting the educational "mess," or the destruction of public education. In such a situation there seems to be no middle or common ground in which cooler heads can unite.

The shrillness of these policy disputes reduces the emphasis on finding rational, balanced solutions. Political ideology and a zero-sum approach to politics and policy became the order of the day.

Certainly, there has been no end to ideology since the beginning of the 1980s, as some believed was occurring in the 1970s. Instead "Reaganomics" contributed to a widening gap between the rich and the poor and this seemed to exacerbate partisan debate and further stymie governmental action. In 1992, controversies over health care—lack of coverage for millions and skyrocketing costs—illustrate the wide gap in the way Republicans and Democrats approach public policy controversies. The Reagan "revolution" was based on a definite and clear ideological preference for a certain approach to public policy in general: eliminate government regulation, reduce taxes, provide tax incentives for business, cut welfare, and privatize the delivery of governmental services. Democrats, of course, did not agree.

This series, Controversial Issues in Public Policy, is meant to shed more light and less ideological heat on major policy issues in the substantive policy areas. In this volume, Alfred A. Marcus begins by describing the "Desert Storm" war with Iraq and the growing U.S. dependence on imported oil. Obviously, this is a major issue for the United States, as its economic base is so heavily tied to adequate supplies of petroleum. Dependence on petroleum and the failure of the country to develop alternative sources of energy are also very controversial issues addressed by Marcus.

The United States is not alone in being heavily dependent on petroleum: Japan and Great Britain are in the same boat, and Marcus describes how these countries, as well as France and the European Economic Community, are reacting to the global energy crisis.

Is nuclear energy a viable alternative? Marcus describes the history of the development of nuclear energy in the United States and concludes with the following assessment: "As more plants were built and they grew in size and complexity, scientific uncertainty surrounding nuclear power increased, regulatory requirements became more stringent and cumbersome, and the costs escalated to the point where nuclear power was even less competitive with alternative means for generating electricity than it had been at the outset."

Marcus's major contribution is in placing controversies in energy policy in a global economic as well as political context. We believe that he has clearly analyzed energy controversies without falling into ideological polemics.

RITA MAE KELLY
DENNIS PALUMBO

Preface

You wake up in the morning and find the following headline in your newspaper: "Iraq Takes Control in Kuwait: Bush Embargoes Trade, Won't Rule Out Military Role." Your heart sinks as you wonder what this development will mean. The world economy depends for its very existence on stable supplies of realistically priced energy. In an increasingly interdependent world, no nation is self-sufficient. The leading economies in the world—the United States, Japan, and Western Europe—require energy from highly unstable areas of the globe whose leaders have been prone to take rash action with unpredictable consequences. In the last 20 years major energy price shocks in 1973 and 1979 shook the world. With the decline of the cold war, energy policy issues, with their focal point in the Persian Gulf, are among the most important factors in world politics. Not that they supersede global trade, the opening up of the economies of the Eastern bloc, or emerging environmental problems, but rather that they provide for these and other issues a new context for their evolution.

A key long-term challenge that the world faces is to break the link between economic growth and oil consumption. In so doing it would become less vulnerable to supply interruptions. The relationships between the economy and energy consumption, however, are extremely complicated, as I will show in this book. Obtaining a better understanding of these relationships is my primary aim. The ways in which we have coped with past energy shocks reveal both the shortcomings and failures and some surprising successes. Lessons can be learned so that mistakes will not be repeated.

The role that governments and markets play in determining how nations cope with energy supply interruptions will be examined here. Both markets and governments have useful roles to play in bringing about adjustments to altered energy conditions. Markets are the main factor motivating people to change their behavior, but markets not properly corrected by governments to reflect the full social costs of energy use cannot possibly do their job. Insofar as energy prices fail to reflect the environmental damage and the national security burdens of energy use, governments will continue to play a useful role in adjusting energy prices.

Instead of acting to keep prices artificially low, governments should impose taxes on energy use. This idea appears to be a universal panacea that will spur conservation, reduce pollution, stimulate the search for alternative technologies, and help reduce trade and budget deficits. Negative redistributional consequences are no reason for its nonadoption, as additional government revenues earned from energy taxes can aid the poor. The real question is why politicians have been so loath to accept the idea. Does the U.S. Bill of Rights guarantee low energy prices? For in comparison to all countries in the world, energy prices in the United States truly are low. A gallon of gas in other industrialized nations costs two to three times the U.S. price, and most of the differences lies in energy taxes (see Tables 1 and 2).

I will introduce the current energy issues by reviewing the events that transpired in the Persian Gulf after August 1990. I will then examine trends in energy production and consumption in the United States and in the world since the first energy supply shock of 1973. Great strides ultimately were made in coping with earlier supply interruptions, but these adjustments were neither smooth, quick, nor without damage to the world economy. The peak in the adjustment process, moreover, was reached in 1986: Growing demand and weakened supply, in addition to rapidly changing geopolitical conditions and festering Arab resentments, made the world particularly vulnerable to upheaval by 1990.

A discussion of the economics and the politics of energy policy follows. Economic doctrine maintains that in the long term energy

Table 1 Percentage of Taxes in Gasoline Prices

	1980	*1982*	*1984*	*1986*	*1988*	*1989*	*1990*	*1991*
Australia	18.7	17.0	24.6	41.0	47.0	48.4	44.9	53.1
Austria	41.6	44.8	49.9	57.3	61.7	58.5	56.0	58.1
Belgium	53.3	52.2	55.2	63.8	65.3	65.2	65.4	66.5
Canada	24.5	26.3	25.0	33.0	39.2	42.7	42.4	42.2
Denmark	58.8	53.3	57.3	71.0	76.2	73.0	69.1	67.8
Finland	36.1	32.2	34.0	46.7	53.5	52.4	55.3	61.3
France	58.0	52.7	57.3	73.9	77.0	74.6	74.2	75.0
Germany	48.7	48.1	48.7	61.5	64.3	65.0	63.1	67.6
Greece	41.8	34.6	47.1	68.1	67.4	55.8	63.8	n.a.
Ireland	48.1	50.1	56.5	65.8	70.7	69.1	67.1	66.2
Italy	61.4	59.5	65.6	78.2	78.7	75.9	75.0	76.0
Japan	36.7	32.9	37.2	43.9	46.6	47.1	45.6	45.7
Luxembourg	43.8	43.0	44.2	53.5	57.7	54.9	54.4	54.9
Netherlands	52.3	48.8	56.0	66.7	70.6	67.6	66.0	70.0
New Zealand	27.6	21.9	21.5	30.9	50.3	47.0	45.7	45.7
Norway	51.7	48.1	50.3	60.6	67.0	62.7	62.9	67.4
Portugal	61.4	57.5	53.7	67.6	68.6	65.0	67.8	72.2
Spain	34.6	30.8	39.2	67.6	65.9	64.3	63.0	65.4
Sweden	49.3	42.8	42.7	56.7	62.2	59.1	65.5	67.7
Switzerland	51.1	48.2	49.5	61.3	64.7	60.7	59.2	59.5
Turkey	n.a.	n.a.	n.a.	n.a.	n.a.	52.2	53.0	56.1
United Kingdom	46.3	54.2	54.9	63.9	67.1	63.6	62.2	66.0
United States	11.2	12.0	23.8	32.7	31.2	29.3	26.7	32.9

supply shortages cannot hold, for with enough time, a commodity in scarce supply becomes more expensive. Higher prices hasten the discovery of new supplies. People adapt through conservation, switching to alternatives, and technological innovations. The negative impact of supply interruptions is in the short term. I will present evidence on the effects of past supply shocks on economic growth, inflation, and employment in the United States and the world. The slowdown in world economic growth that coincided with the period of the 1973 and 1979 supply shocks is at least partially a consequence of these events. The lesson that emerges from this examination of the economics of energy policy is that if governments do not intervene to maintain artificially low energy prices, markets can effectively achieve long-term adjustments. In the short term, however, markets are likely to have less impact because of rigidities in people's habits and ways of behaving and

Table 2 Gasoline Prices in US Dollars/Liter

	1980	*1982*	*1984*	*1986*	*1988*	*1989*	*1990*	*1991*
Australia	0.347	0.392	0.417	0.347	0.416	0.437	0.512	0.457
Austria	0.670	0.662	0.570	0.624	0.725	0.729	0.904	0.842
Belgium	0.790	0.653	0.551	0.572	0.673	0.697	0.912	0.916
Canada	0.223	0.362	0.390	0.347	0.407	0.432	0.496	0.505
Denmark	0.804	0.712	0.578	0.794	0.970	0.937	1.013	0.946
Finland	0.776	0.722	0.633	0.621	0.800	0.822	1.089	1.093
France	0.799	0.674	0.590	0.680	0.808	0.812	0.981	0.950
Germany	0.640	0.573	0.492	0.496	0.581	0.656	0.791	0.866
Greece	0.815	0.654	0.490	0.557	0.544	0.475	0.727	0.755
Ireland	0.653	0.733	0.677	0.792	0.880	0.870	1.033	1.006
Italy	0.817	0.761	0.734	0.858	1.045	1.003	1.233	1.238
Japan	0.648	0.658	0.610	0.730	0.905	0.863	0.858	0.944
Luxembourg	0.610	0.547	0.463	0.469	0.577	0.572	0.681	0.661
Netherlands	0.721	0.652	0.563	0.608	0.796	0.782	0.959	0.999
New Zealand	0.478	0.515	0.451	0.432	0.587	0.538	0.574	0.577
Norway	0.752	0.714	0.638	0.644	0.822	0.838	1.018	1.118
Portugal	0.870	0.759	0.647	0.761	0.827	0.792	0.959	1.018
Spain	0.753	0.647	0.578	0.586	0.652	0.646	0.807	0.854
Sweden	0.697	0.631	0.510	0.583	0.729	0.746	1.090	1.123
Switzerland	0.688	0.621	0.515	0.562	0.654	0.646	0.784	0.771
Turkey	0.630	0.596	0.485	0.451	0.408	0.477	0.624	0.735
United Kingdom	0.658	0.640	0.541	0.550	0.668	0.662	0.785	0.851
United States	0.329	0.342	0.320	0.245	0.250	0.270	0.307	0.301

because of difficulties in replacing the durable capital investments (such as cars and buildings) that people have to consume energy.

I then turn from the role of markets to that of governments. In particular, I will trace the contradictory policies carried out by the U.S. government after the supply shocks of 1973 and 1979. These policies prevented energy prices from rising, thereby slowing changes that otherwise would have taken place. If prices had been allowed to rise, the U.S. adjustment to earlier energy shocks would have been more rapid. Government policies blunted the impact of the supply interruptions at a cost to the U.S. and world economies. U.S. policymakers increased demand for energy even as they tried to encourage conservation and the development of alternative supplies. Given these contradictory purposes, the efforts were self-defeating. I will examine why the policies nonetheless were carried out. In politics, pure efficiency is not the only important value. U.S. politicians balanced what they thought to be equity and fairness along with efficiency in producing the contradictory policies the United States pursued.

The policies of the U.S. government in coping with the supply interruptions cannot be understood in isolation from the policies of other participants in the international economy. We will look at the role of these participants, specifically the major supplier of the world's petroleum—the Organization of Petroleum Exporting Countries (OPEC)—and some of the major users of this petroleum, including Japan and the countries in Western Europe. How OPEC was formed, what it has done, and what it has failed to do will be examined in light of the economic theory of cartels. Then the role of major consuming nations outside the United States will be considered. The United States along with Canada is the most profligate user of energy in the world. In Japan and some Western European nations, demand for and supply of energy are very different, and these nations have been more successful at reducing their energy use. Different policies have also been pursued in these nations, as I will note.

I end with an assessment of two energy technologies—shale oil and nuclear power—which, although very different, are often considered to be promising alternatives to petroleum. The historical experience with these technologies is fairly typical of the historical experience with other technological alternatives, e.g. photovoltaics (see Appendix 1). The promise of these technologies along with the pitfalls in their development will be considered. Again, understanding the role of governments and markets is critical. Governments and markets provide the context for the development of these technologies; they have at different times and in different ways both promoted and stifled their development. The history of U.S. involvement in shale oil production and nuclear power illustrates this thesis. Federal enthusiasm for these energy types, as well as their market appeal, waxed and waned. In the final chapter of the book, the challenges that the electric utility industry faces in responding to rapidly changing energy conditions are discussed; the role that nuclear power plays in this industry is also explored.

Energy policy has broad ramifications and thus it has been hard to circumscribe the limits of this book. I have attempted to cover the economics and politics of energy policies as they have emerged in the United States and elsewhere in the world in light of the major disturbances in energy prices that the world has faced. Worldwide comparisons demonstrate that there are significant differences in the way nations and societies cope with energy crises, and that these differences have important implications. Alternative technologies to petroleum are considered—a focus at the end of the book is the decisions that have to be made by the electric power industry about nuclear power and other forms of power generation. I have only been able to touch briefly on the national security issues that affect the energy question, including the Persian Gulf and Middle Eastern politics that are ever more critical to energy policy. Other important elements, which I have been unable to consider here, are the trade-offs between energy and environmental policies and the importance of technological developments and innovation in solving energy problems.

In the long run energy and environmental problems will be solved by technological developments and innovation. Wise governments will make sure that prices provide true signals to markets to stimulate these developments. Prices must reflect the full social costs of energy production. When they do, the market itself will compel people to conserve, innovate, and find alternatives to using fossil fuels obtainable only from politically unstable regions of the globe.

PART I

1

An Introduction to Energy Policy
The Crisis in the Gulf

With the benefit of hindsight it is easy to see that something ominous was likely to happen in the Persian Gulf. In spring 1990 it already was apparent that U.S. production of crude oil was falling dramatically and alternative production methods and technologies, although promising, were hardly ready to take up the slack. Moreover, Saddam Hussein of Iraq was taking actions that were shifting the geopolitical balance and making demands that might shift the balance even further. The United States was distracted, its attention diverted by changes in the Soviet Union and looming budget battles only peripherally related to the energy situation. OPEC meanwhile was unraveling. Oil prices had been declining because OPEC had been unable to enforce its production quotas (Sullivan, 1990c). This state of affairs was not to the liking of Saddam Hussein, who needed cash to rebuild his war-torn economy. Using the pretext of long-standing disagreements with Kuwait, he launched a brutal invasion of that country ("Iraqi invasion raises oil prices," 1990). The world responded with indignation, condemning Iraq and imposing an economic boycott. War began shortly thereafter. But after the United States and its allies achieved a stunning military victory, important questions remained about the political settlements that would follow the war. In this chapter, I will trace the developments that led to and culminated in the crisis in the gulf, a crisis of great importance in the history of energy policy.

Declining U.S. Production

In spring 1990, U.S. oil production was declining ("Rising oil import bill," 1990). Output from the Alaskan North Slope had peaked at about 2 million barrels a day in 1988, and production of domestic crude oil, 7.6 million barrels a day, was at a 26-year low. In 1989 only 542 exploratory wells had been dug, a decline from 2,334 in 1984. Because of restrictions on drilling offshore or in Alaskan wildlife preserves, the drilling taking place was in areas where less oil was likely to be discovered. The implications of this decline in U.S. production were ominous. In March 1990 it was reported that the U.S. bill for imported oil in 1989 had increased by 28%. This rapidly growing bill for imported oil hindered efforts to close the trade deficit. Nearly $50 billion of the trade deficit, or about 45%, was money spent on foreign oil. The United States imported 46% of the oil it consumed in 1989, substantially more than the 31.5% it imported in 1985 and very near the 1977 record of 47.7%. The Department of Energy (DOE) estimated that by the year 2000 domestic production would fall to under 6 million barrels per day and the bill for imported oil would increase to over $100 billion per year in constant dollars if oil prices increased as anticipated to nearly $28 a barrel. The United States would be importing over 75% of the oil it consumed. For a nation that imported very little petroleum prior to 1970, this change was remarkable.

Exotic alternatives to imported oil were not showing much promise, and thus the long-term prospects for escaping heavy dependence on foreign oil did not seem particularly good. As an example, there was cold fusion, the possibility of extracting vast sums of energy from the forging together of subatomic material (Broad, 1990). Cold fusion was the ultimate in the exotic alternatives, with commercial prospects likely only in the distant future. Still, it offered immense promise of cheap and abundant power that would virtually eliminate world dependence on petroleum from politically unstable regions. But scientists were having trouble confirming the claims of University of Utah chemists of obtaining from cold fusion devices 17 to 40 times the amount of energy introduced electrically. The positive results the Utah chemists reported could not be reproduced on demand. Bursts of energy would suddenly turn on and turn off, and the scientists had no understanding of why. Moreover, they detected no radioactive traces to show that a nuclear reaction actually had taken place.

From where was future U.S. energy going to come? (Solomon, 1990). To revive old domestic petroleum fields, oil companies were getting ready to expand the use of methods such as horizontal drilling to enable them to capture oil that had been trapped on levels that could not be reached by conventional methods. Although the costs of horizontal drilling were about twice the costs of a conventional well, production rates could be four to five times as great, so that the expenses could be rapidly recovered (in the best of cases within a year). The 1989-1990 market for horizontal drilling equipment increased 18 times from what it had been in 1988-1989. Independent oil companies such as Oryx Energy, Union Pacific Resources, and Burlington Resources took the lead in using this new method. Some of the large integrated companies like ARCO, Amoco, and Texaco also used the method, but to a lesser extent. Horizontal drilling had the potential to revive moribund fields in Colorado, North Dakota, and Wyoming, the payoff being that the United States could increase its proven reserves, considered to be about 27 billion barrels, by several billion barrels. But even an increase of several billion barrels did not put the United States anywhere near the Persian Gulf powers in the capability to supply the world with oil.

There was no doubt that U.S. oil vulnerabilities, which started with the import of substantial amounts of foreign petroleum, again were rising. Iraq began to lay the groundwork for exploiting these vulnerabilities, holding direct talks with the Iran aimed at resolving the remaining issues in the decade-old hostility between the two nations. While the Bush administration concentrated on upcoming budget talks, which were likely to be protracted and complicated, Iraq and Iran focused on the decisions that would have to be made by the Organization of Petroleum Exporting Countries (OPEC) to continue the efforts begun in the early 1970s to limit the amount of oil sold on world markets in order to maintain prices. The views of Iraq and Iran converged on the issues OPEC was confronting (How big an oil schock?, 1990). Both countries wanted higher oil prices and lower production levels in order to earn more foreign currency to help rebuild their war-shattered economies. To accomplish these purposes, they felt that Saudi Arabian power had to diminish in both regional politics and OPEC. In their view, the Saudis, the holders of the world's largest oil reserves, along with the oil sheikdoms in the Persian Gulf, such as Kuwait, the United Arab Emirates, and Oman, were acting in concert with the United States to keep oil prices low.

Among the items the Bush administration was considering to reduce the budget deficit was a broad-based energy tax calculated by the Btu (British thermal unit) and affecting nearly every energy source from gasoline, oil, natural gas, and nuclear to hydroelectric power ("Energy taxes for America," 1990). This tax would mean an increase of about 5 to 6 cents in the price of a gallon of gas in addition to the existing federal gas tax of 9 cents a gallon. The tax would bring an additional $20 billion to the federal treasury, about 40% of the reduction in the budget deficit that was needed. At the time, such a tax did not seem out of line, with the fuel cost of a mile's driving in the United States having plunged to 2 cents in 1989 from 4 cents in 1979. An energy tax would reduce the budget and trade deficits and by discouraging energy use also help the environment. The biggest cause of pollution is energy use, which contributes to oil spills, acid rain, smog, and global greenhouse warming. The tax, which would also encourage conservation and the development of alternative fuels and technologies, was favored by some Democrats because of the environmental benefits, but bitterly resisted by other Democrats who claimed that the burden would fall most heavily on the poor.

The next turn of events, the unraveling of OPEC, provided the context for the situation to further deteriorate. Oil prices had plummeted from $22 a barrel in January 1990 to $16 in July 1990 as OPEC producers brought nearly 3 million extra barrels of oil a day into inventories in the second quarter of 1990. Prices for low-grade crude slipped below $10 a barrel for a period (Tanner, 1990a). The 13 member states of OPEC reported revenues declining at a rate of $100 million a day. Iraq claimed that it lost $1 billion a year for every dollar reduction in the price of a barrel of oil. There were fears among the OPEC nations that prices would drop further, even as low as $7 a barrel. Iraq, along with Venezuela and Indonesia, blamed the weak petroleum markets on Kuwait and the United Arab Emirates, whom they accused of cheating on production quotas. Iraq had little faith in Saudi Arabia, which was trying to mediate the situation, searching for a new strategy to get Kuwait and the United Arab Emirates to cut back on production. Reflecting the widespread uncertainty, the future price of crude oil for August crept up, but only by 11 cents a barrel, to $16.58 on the New York Mercantile Exchange.

Iraq's debt from its war with Iran was an immense $80 billion, and it wanted to see oil prices go up to $25 a barrel both to pay this debt and to fund continued military expansion. Kuwait, however, held diversified investments in the West and did not want to see the world economy, already tottering on the edge, slip into recession on account of high oil prices. Kuwait sought a stable oil price of about $14. The dispute between the two nations over oil prices opened an old rift between them (Brooks & Horwitz, 1990). Lacking an outlet to the sea, Iraq had been demanding from Kuwait the lease of Bubiyan Island, an empty sandbank at the head of the Persian Gulf. This territorial dispute was only part of the reason that the two nations were at odds. More fundamental was Iraq's Baathist ideology, which committed it to a pan-Arabism that did not recognize the territorial integrity of neighboring Arab states.

In response to the Iraqi inspired demands, OPEC agreed to a new oil price floor of $21 a barrel, based on a production limit of 22.5 million barrels. Iraq, however, was not satisfied. In summer 1990, to push oil prices up to the agreed-upon $21 a barrel would have been difficult because petroleum inventories in the world were large and consumption lagging—world consumption had increased only 1% in 1990, and in the United States, the world's largest consumer of energy, it had declined 2%. Kuwait responded to the situation by affirming its acceptance of the OPEC oil production quota and agreeing to negotiate its border dispute with Iraq. Kuwait was part of the Gulf Cooperation Council (GCC), which included Saudi Arabia, Bahrain, Qatar, Oman, and the United Arab Emirates. Neither Kuwait nor its allies in the GCC had the military capacity of defending themselves in a military confrontation with Iraq, and when Iraqi troops moved to the Kuwaiti border, the gulf sheikhdoms looked to the United States for protection.

The Iraqi Invasion

With the unraveling of OPEC, the reopening of Iraqi claims, and the military maneuvers, tensions were building, but few expected the Iraqi takeover of Kuwait. With Kuwaiti reserves about 10% of the world total and Iraqi reserves another 10%, Iraq now held more than 20% of world reserves under its control. Moreover, it threatened the oil resources of the remaining Gulf states, which together constituted nearly 70% of the world total. The condemnation of the Iraqi action brought together nations that previously had been adversaries, including the United States and the Soviet Union. It united the moderate Arab states of Egypt and Saudi Arabia with hard-line and intransigent Syria, Iraq's traditional foe. Certainly, Iraq faced difficult economic circumstances at home—an inflation rate estimated at 22% in 1988, a decline in the gross domestic product (GDP) of 4%, and the huge foreign debts that were the legacy the 10-year war with Iran; but in attacking Kuwait, Saddam Hussein was shaking the economic security of all nations. With nearly 70% of the world's proven oil reserves, the Persian Gulf supplied more than a quarter of the world's daily need for oil, powering the world's automobiles and factories. Forty-seven percent of the oil used in Europe came from the Persian Gulf. Sixty-three percent of the oil used in Japan came from the Persian Gulf. If Saddam Hussein became master of the Gulf, he would be virtually free to determine how much of this oil was to be supplied, to whom, and at what price.

World oil prices skyrocketed after the invasion of Kuwait, moving to $27 a barrel the next day (Greenhouse, 1990; Solomon, 1990; Tanner 1990d). Each $4 increase in the cost of a barrel of crude oil raised U.S. gasoline prices about 10 cents a gallon. Industries like airlines, chemicals, and steel, which were heavy users of petroleum and petroleum by-products, quickly suffered. For instance, for each penny change in the price per gallon of jet fuel, United Airlines's annual expenses went up by $22.5 million (Medina, 1990). U.S. automobile manufacturers, spurred on toward larger, more powerful, less fuel-efficient cars by relatively low gas prices since 1986, would lose ground to Japanese competitors. Although Japanese manufacturers consistently achieved average fuel efficiency standards of over 30 miles per gallon (mpg), the U.S. car manufacturers were stuck at about 27 mpg. According to Environmental Protection Agency (EPA) estimates, 9 of the 10 most fuel-efficient 1991 model cars were made in Japan. The 10th was not a U.S. car either, but the Volkswagen Jetta.

In many ways Japan was better prepared to deal with this oil price jolt than the United States (Chandler & Brauchli, 1990). By energy conservation and industrial restructuring, Japan had reduced energy use to the point where it was producing 2.24 times the real output for the same energy input as in 1973. Although nearly 80% of its total energy supplies in 1973 came from oil, by 1990 this figure dropped to under 58%. The United States used about 2.5 times the amount of energy per person for commercial purposes as Japan. A dollar a barrel increase in oil prices would increase the U.S. trade deficit by $2.9 billion annually, but would only reduce Japan's trade surplus by $1.3 billion a year. And a 10% increase in the price of oil was likely to add 0.6 percentage points to the U.S. inflation rate, but only 0.2 percentage points to the Japanese inflation rate.

All but one of the eight post-World War II U.S. recessions had been preceded by an oil price shock (Anderson, Bryan, & Pike, 1990). The U.S. economy already was tottering on the edge with consumer confidence down and factory orders declining (Murray & Wessel, 1990). If the Federal Reserve increased the money supply and lowered interest rates, it risked exacerbating inflation, as happened in the 1970s after the first oil price shock when loose monetary policies helped raise inflation to double-digit levels. The Dow-Jones average tumbled, losing 183 points in just 3 days following the invasion. Some analysts estimated oil prices would rise as high as $50 or $60 a barrel.

The United States, nearly 50% dependent on foreign supplies, obtained about 6.6% of its imported oil from Iraq and about 1.5% from Kuwait. The largest foreign suppliers to the United States were Venezuela, Nigeria, and Canada. The Japanese, 99% dependent on foreign oil, imported about 11% of it from Iraq. The countries of the European Economic Community (EEC) imported about 11%. Some of the EEC countries, such as Denmark, obtained more than half of their oil from these sources.

Oil was a pervasive part of the U.S. economy. U.S. fuel and oil costs constituted from 4% to 8% of all shipping costs, in turn affecting food prices as well as the prices of nearly all goods bought and sold. Petroleum-based liquid asphalt was laid on roads and constituted about half the costs of road resurfacing. Raw materials used in adhesives, coatings, and similar products contained petroleum derivatives. Other products that had petroleum derivatives were trash bags and precision plastic parts used in computers. Chemical companies were heavy users of petroleum derivatives. For businesses, the cost increases of the petroleum price rises varied widely depending on the products they made, where in the crude oil production chain these products fell, and how much petro-based material was in the products.

The problem was not that world oil stocks were immediately low; in fact, at the time of the invasion, they were unusually high—around 1.65 billion barrels compared with the usual 1.5 billion ("Oil's economic threat," 1990). The problem was that 60% to 70% of the oil in the world was sold on spot markets where price changes immediately followed forecasts of future availability (Razavi, 1989; Taylor, Nomani, & Angrist, 1990). These markets were extremely volatile and encouraged speculation and hoarding. Between October 1973 and January 1974, when Arab oil producers embargoed oil, the price jumped from $3 to $13 a barrel. The economic effects were a near doubling of the inflation rate in the member states of the Organization for Economic Cooperation and Development (OECD) from 7.9% in 1973 to 14% in 1974 and a reduction in the growth rate of about 1.75%. From the end of 1978 to the end of 1979, oil prices again spiked upward, from $13 a barrel to $39 a barrel. Inflation rates in OECD countries grew from 7.8% at the end of 1978 to 13.6% in the first half of 1980. GNP started to decline in 1979 and did not come back till 1983, as countries in the developed world, determined to fight inflation, let the unemployment rate rise to 8.5%.

As much as the situation in 1990 was similar to the situation during earlier price hikes, it also was different. In 1973, when Arab oil producers refused to ship oil to the United States, Japan, and other Western nations, Saudi Arabia, along with OPEC, was an instigator and supporter of the boycott. Now it was not OPEC, but the United Nations, by virtue of a 13-0 Security Council vote, that decided to impose widespread trade restrictions on Iraq. The Saudis supported the effort with the promise of 2 million extra barrels of oil a day to replenish world supplies (Tanner, Murray, & Rosewicz, 1990)—about half what the world would need to completely make up for 20% of its supply lost from Iraq and Kuwait (Tanner, 1990a).

Other differences between 1990 and earlier oil shocks existed. U.S. dependence on OPEC oil was now greater (28% in 1990 compared to about 13% in 1974), but in general the industrialized nations had diversified their sources of energy. In 1974 about a half of the world's oil came from OPEC countries, but by 1990 only about one third of the world's oil came from OPEC. Additional production potential had been developed in the North Slope of Alaska, the North Sea, Mexico, and elsewhere (Sullivan, 1990b). Earlier oil crises had motivated industrial nations to improve the efficiency with which they used petroleum to the point where in 1990 they used 40% less oil to produce a dollar of real GNP.

The United States and other nations had large oil reserves that could last for as much as 200 days (Biddle, 1990). The United States with its 590-million-barrel oil reserve, the Japanese with their 140-million-barrel reserve, and the Germans with their 100-million-barrel reserve had prepared for a supply shortage (Solomon & Gutfeld, 1990). The reserves could also be used to steady oil markets. The main problem with the reserves was whether they could be used if they were needed. Two thirds of the petroleum in the U.S. reserve was of the "sour" variety, which was not suitable for many U.S. refineries. It had not been tapped in the past and analysts were uncertain who would buy the oil, what they would do with it, and if there would be hoarding and speculation.

Although the oil-poor underdeveloped countries would suffer, the oil-rich underdeveloped countries would benefit. Mexico and Nigeria would earn currency to pay off their creditors. The Soviet Union was in for a windfall, because as much as two thirds of its foreign currency was earned from energy exports. Rapidly rising oil prices, however, were not in the interests of former Communist nations in Eastern Europe, which imported almost all their oil from the Soviet Union.

In the long term, conservation in conjunction with technological innovation would drive down oil prices (U.S. Congress, Senate Committee on Energy and Natural Resouces, Subcommittee on Energy Regulation and Conservation, 1989, Subcommittee on Energy Research and Development, 1987b, 1988a). High prices could not be sustained. The problem was in the short term: In the short term, alternative supplies were needed, but it was not necessarily easy to find these alternatives.

One supplier of great potential was Mexico (Tanner, 1990d). The full extent of Mexican oil resources was thought to range from 45 billion barrels of oil to 260 billion, but Mexico was ill prepared to provide the world with extra petroleum. Since the debt crisis of 1982, investment in its publicly owned oil company, Pemex, had plummeted, together with drilling. In 1989, Mexico opened only about half the exploratory wells that it did in 1987. Similarly, Canada, once considered a country with oil reserves that had great potential, was having difficulty exploiting these reserves. Its current proven reserves were estimated to be only about 4.2 billion barrels, but it was believed to have vast untapped potential reserves in its northern territories. This oil was not easily accessible, however, and it was proving to be extremely expensive to develop. Canada also had huge deposits of tar sands in its western provinces, but these deposits, a mixture of clay, water, and bitumen, had to be refined before they could be used. This process was not only expensive and capital intensive, but could be extremely damaging to the environment.

The Soviet Union, which produced 20% of the world's oil, could not be called on for additional production because political disruption and outdated technology had ground its oil industry nearly to a halt (Wald,

1990b). Its exports were declining, with chronic shortages of such basic equipment as the pipes and valves essential for a vibrant petroleum industry. Although the Soviet Union had 60 billion barrels of oil reserves, more than twice the amount the United States had, and the Soviet Union also had the world's largest proven natural gas reserves (about 45% of the world's total), it was not likely to add much in the way of new energy production, because it lacked the capability to efficiently produce and market either oil or natural gas (Hewett, 1984; Gumbel & Tanner, 1990).

The U.S. oil industry, too, was in the doldrums. After a century of high production, vast pools of undiscovered oil no longer existed in the United States. Worse still, the infrastructure needed for oil exploration and production had deteriorated in the United States as well as the Soviet Union. For instance, the capability to build pipelines and manufacture drill bits had declined to about 50% of what it had been 10 years earlier. Skilled professional engineers, scientists, and oil field workers were needed to enhance production from existing wells and to find new oil. Many had retired after the last oil boom of the 1970s, and with low oil prices in the 1980s, they had not been replenished. Working in the oil industry with its constant booms and busts simply was not attractive to scientists or to the blue-collar workers who did the hard job of getting the oil out of the ground. Non-OPEC producers such as Mexico, Canada, the Soviet Union, and the United States could be expected to produce at most an additional 200,000 to 400,000 barrels per day.

Besides Saudi Arabia, which was able to take up about half the slack of the oil lost from Iraq and Kuwait, the world could rely on Venezuela for about 600,000 barrels a day and on the United Arab Emirates for about another 800,000 barrels. This left a remaining shortfall of about a half million barrels. As oil prices rose, demand would fall and a variety of producers, notably Nigeria, Indonesia, and Libya, would be willing to make up the difference. As a result, this supply interruption, unlike others in the past, did not involve real shortages of oil.

Yet there was cause for concern in delays in getting the additional production going, as OPEC had to meet and officially agree to the higher production quotas. The first 4 to 6 weeks following the invasion saw the world draw down the large existing reserve. Even after oil started to flow from alternative suppliers, concern remained over a possible winter shortage of about 500,000 barrels a day as demand grew with the cold weather. Another cause for concern was that the Saudi Arabian and Venezuelan oil that replaced the Iraqi and Kuwaiti oil was of the heavy variety and could not be refined as easily or put to the same uses.

The Need for an Energy Policy

Clearly, the United States, both in the interim and for the long term, needed an energy policy to reduce its dependence on foreign oil. It had made substantial progress in reducing this dependence between 1976 to 1986, when it cut its ratio of energy use to GNP by 2.8% per year, but by 1987 this progress had come to a halt. Much of the improvement came about because the United States had eased out of energy-intensive heavy industries, exporting them abroad and replacing them with service industries that used less energy. Progress also took place because automobiles obtained 50% more miles per gallon than in 1973. But the improvements in auto efficiency reversed as post-1985 gasoline prices dipped to inflation-adjusted lows. With cheaper driving possible, people were driving more (Wald, 1990b).

Americans on average used more gasoline than people in other countries with comparable standards of living, or about 350 gallons per person in 1989. For comparison, West Germans consumed only about 150 gallons—not because the West Germans had more efficient vehicles, but because Americans drove more miles and had more cars. In the United States as well as the rest of the world, the ratio of cars per person was rising.

The Bush administration resisted the idea of mounting a major conservation effort (Krauss, 1990). It wanted to handle the crisis differently and avoid reminding people of the sacrifices they had been asked to make during the Carter years. The administration's first stab at devising a policy relied solely on voluntary cooperation. It put inflating automobile tires to their optimal pressure at the head of a list of conservation measures—an admittedly weak and ineffectual gesture, but the administration claimed savings of 100,000 barrels of oil a day if drivers carried it out. Other measures included advocating increased car and van pooling. With 20% more ride sharing, the administration claimed that another 90,000 barrels of oil could be saved. It also called on people to observe speed limits, which could save 50,000 barrels a day, and for those with a choice to drive their most energy efficient car, saving 40,000 barrels a day.

To increase supply, administration officials asked oil companies to produce additional oil from the Alaskan North Slope. They also considered reopening the Arctic National Wildlife Refuge for exploration, closed in the aftermath of the *Exxon Valdez* oil spill. DOE offered to mediate a dispute that was preventing oil from being produced off the California coast. A consortium led by Chevron could pump up to 100,000 barrels a day from platforms already built near Santa Barbara, but it was being denied permits on environmental grounds by state and local authorities. DOE in addition announced that it would switch its own vehicles to gasohol—a blend of gasoline and 10% ethanol—and would encourage ethanol producers to produce at full capacity. The administration called on industries to switch from petroleum to more plentiful natural gas wherever possible. Overall, these programs were designed to increase U.S. supply by 270,000 barrels a day.

The Bush administration was reluctant to do more. There were a variety of reasons, including its free market ideology; public opinion polls showing that other options were unpopular; and domestic political interests, agitated about the budget deficit and ready to exact a high price for any additional steps the administration might take. On the grounds that the government should not intervene in energy markets, the administration opposed a bill introduced in Congress by Senator Richard Bryan, a Democrat from Nevada, that would have forced auto manufacturers to improve fleet fuel efficiency standards to 40 mpg by the year 2001 (Gutfeld, 1990). The bill, initially designed as an environmental measure to prevent the escape of greenhouse gases into the atmosphere, would have saved 2.8 million barrels of oil per day by the year 2005, more than all the oil the United States had been importing from the Persian Gulf. Energy secretary James Watkins admitted that two thirds of the oil burned each day in the United States was for transportation, the largest share by the 171 million private cars and trucks, but he stressed that most auto manufacturers opposed the bill on the grounds that the public was demanding larger, that is "safer," cars, which would be impossible to build if the bill took effect (Gutfield, 1990). The administration supported the auto industry claims with studies asserting that the proposal would result in additional highway accidents and deaths. William Reilly, EPA administrator, wrote a letter opposing the bill. On September 25, 1990, lawmakers who supported the bill lost a procedural vote in the Senate, ending hope for the bill's passage in 1990 (Gutfield, 1990).

Although 80% of Americans favored tougher conservation measures, when asked if they supported higher gasoline taxes to encourage conservation, 62% were opposed. Despite public opposition, congressional Democrats reintroduced the idea of a tax on energy consumption in the budget talks. The 9-cent-per-gallon tax that they proposed was designed as a revenue-enhancing measure, the purpose of which would be defeated if people actually curtailed their driving. Republicans ultimately accepted this proposal and it became part of the budget agreement, but Congress refused to even consider taking the broader step of gradually increasing U.S. gasoline taxes to levels prevailing in other industrialized countries. In France, England, West Germany, and Japan, it was routine for motorists to spend $45 to $50 to fill their tanks with gas. More than 75% of this expense was in the form of taxes. The idea of adjusting markets to reflect the true social costs of petroleum use was not one that was accepted by either Congress or the administration.

Other opinions expressed by the U.S. public made it difficult to develop a more elaborate energy policy. In a poll taken August 23, 1990, 57% of Americans, despite the Persian Gulf crisis, continued to oppose the construction of more nuclear power plants, and only 48% favored easing restrictions on offshore oil drilling (Greenhouse, 1990). Tax breaks to stimulate the oil industry were out of the question given the size of the budget deficit as well as windfall profits for the oil industry from high petroleum prices. Solar power obtained a boost with a congressionally sponsored and administration-endorsed 30% increase in research funding, but this increase appeared insignificant compared with the funding for solar power in countries such as Japan. The Bush administration considered a tax credit for alternative energy investments—which was supported by environmentalists—but economists in the administration warned that such measures would not result in sufficient additional investments to justify the budgetary costs.

In a famous gesture designed for direct comparison with the Carter administration, Bush continued to use a gas-guzzling motorboat during his summer holiday in Maine. On August 31, 1990, the administration announced its support of the first national advertising campaign in a decade to promote conservation. It was also considering a tax credit designed to stimulate the recovery of hard-to-get oil from existing fields and a plan to expedite the permitting process for oil exploration in the Beaufort Sea off Alaska. Bush went so far as to declare that the United States "must never again enter any crisis—economic or military—with an excessive dependence on foreign oil" (Greenhouse, 1990). But he took no further action to back up his words.

The U.S. government hesitated, but the Japanese government did not. It had no reason not to show its people that it believed that this oil crisis was as serious as earlier ones. The corridors of government buildings again were dark, and air conditioners were turned down in offices, making them uncomfortably hot in August 1990. Japan's giant Ministry of Trade and Industry (MITI) prohibited drivers' exceeding 50 miles per hour and buildings cooler than 28°C. MITI reaffirmed its commitment to the intensive conservation programs it had initiated following the 1979 oil price hike. Since 1979 it had kept close tabs on the energy consumption of nearly 5,000 factories, requiring from 1 to 10 energy conservation engineers on selected factory floors. The engineers had to spend up to a year studying for an exam so rigorous that 80% failed. Those who passed were charged with taking concrete steps to make Japanese factories more energy efficient and made reports about daily energy use to MITI.

MITI also encouraged companies to switch from oil to coal and natural gas, available from politically stable nations. And it allowed oil and gas companies as well as the utilities that supplied electricity to keep their prices artificially high so long as they diverted the excess profit to energy research. In essence, this created an energy tax in Japan with many important benefits. Raising energy prices had the effect of not only stimulating energy research but also discouraging energy use. In 1987 the tax was used for more than $830 million in energy research, which helped Japan develop the world's most advanced solar cell technology, the world's best means for transporting and storing liquid natural gas, and new methods for producing electricity from gasified coal and seawater.

Japanese efforts following the 1973 and 1979 oil shocks insulated it to a much greater extent than other countries from energy price hikes (Chandler & Brauchli, 1990). The oil share of total Japanese energy demand dropped from 77% in 1973 to 57% in 1987, despite the fact that individual Japanese consumers became wealthier and bought more TV sets, refrigerators, air conditioners, and other appliances. Japanese also drove more and bought more cars. The main reduction in energy use took place in industry, and two factors were important in bringing about the change—the previously mentioned energy conservation engineers program, which showed that the government was serious about conservation, and the tax on energy that provided a concrete incentive for change. Numerous examples can be found of companies that invested heavily to reduce energy use. Nippon Steel Company installed a coke dry quencher, a piece of equipment costing $5.6 million, that cut energy use by 25%. Asahi Glass rebuilt production equipment and redesigned production processes to cut energy use 40% over a decade. Japan's northern subway system recycled heat from engines for use in air conditioning to save energy. Hino Motors added switches to its machine tools so that they would not idle when not in use. It recycled machine oil and reduced shop lighting and air conditioning. Tokyo Electric Power Company converted to nuclear power, cutting its use of oil by two thirds. In 1990 Japan's 38 nuclear power plants supplied 9% of the country's total energy needs, an increase from nearly zero in 1973. Geographic compactness, population density, and superior public transportation offered Japan advantages the United States lacked. Like the United States, Japan also benefited from a movement away from energy-intensive hard industry toward financial services and consumer electronics that used much less energy. Nonetheless, Japan, already more energy efficient than the United States in 1973, improved its efficiency by one third, even though the additional progress was very hard to make. Between 1973 and 1987, Japanese economic output more than doubled, but its reliance on oil imports fell by 25%. U.S. reliance on foreign imports actually increased during this period, from 36% to 43% of total oil consumed.

Long-Term Energy Alternatives

In the long run there are options offering great promise for the United States or any country willing to take advantage of them (Sullivan, 1990b). Perpetual heavy reliance on imported oil from unstable regions is neither necessary nor inevitable.

With 4,000 trillion cubic feet of gas reserves underground in the United States, Canada, and other countries, natural gas is far more plentiful than oil. Another benefit is that it is cleaner burning and less polluting. But additional conversion in the United States of industries from oil to natural gas has been limited to about the equivalent of 160,000 barrels of oil a day. The extent to which natural gas is an attractive auto fuel replacement depends on its price and whether it can be adapted for use in internal combustion engines. As oil prices rose, natural gas prices also went up. Existing cars could run on natural gas if engine modifications were made and a compressed-gas storage tank added. If natural gas prices rose too rapidly, however, the conversion of existing autos would not be worth it. Another problem with natural gas is greater difficulty in storage and transport. Thus it is not a practical replacement for gasoline. Mobil Corporation developed an advanced process at its New Zealand subsidiary to convert natural gas directly to gasoline at a price just under $35 a barrel. The New Zealand plant produced 15,000 barrels of gasoline a day, providing one third of New Zealand's needs.

An even better alternative from an environmental perspective is conservation—the option the Bush administration slighted in its initial plan but that proved so successful for the Japanese. The Bush administration was correct in its assessment that official government programs to encourage conservation did not work as well as simple price increases. Historically, for every 10% rise in fuel prices, people used 2% less oil. A 30% drop in consumption following the previous energy price hike took place because people decreased energy use in response to the higher prices. The potential for reduced energy use was great. People had been increasing energy use in the 1980s because energy prices had fallen. On average, Americans in 1990 drove 1,000 more miles per year than they did in 1980. Since 1987, the cars they used were 7% heavier, 10% more powerful, and half a mile per gallon less fuel efficient. Simply reversing these trends could mean saving 200,000 barrels of oil a day.

An increase in oil prices would compel U.S. airlines to lower consumption (Medina, 1990). Next to labor, jet fuel was the biggest expense for the airlines. Jumbo jets averaged less than half a mile per gallon, making the average fuel cost of a flight from New York to Los Angeles $7,000. Greater fuel costs pushed the airlines toward record losses of over $1 billion in 1990. To cut energy consumption they called on pilots to fly at higher altitudes where the air is thinner and to take the most direct route between locations, even if the flight was somewhat more choppy for passengers. A light touch on the throttle once the plane was at cruising speed was also recommended, and pilots were asked not to keep engines idling at airports, even if it meant shutting off air conditioners and inconveniencing passengers.

Immediately after the Iraqi invasion, high fuel prices, along with a looming recession, depressed energy consumption in industrial countries (Tanner, 1990c). In response to higher energy prices—or the anticipation of them—people chose to conserve. Oil demand in the 24 nations that make up the OECD declined by 400,000 barrels of oil a day, or 1%, in the third quarter of 1990. Only the fast-growing Asian economies experienced increases, and these were small. The flattening of world oil demand delayed shortages that might have arisen from the Persian Gulf crisis. In fact, with petroleum demand sluggish, the effort by leading OPEC states, such as Saudi Arabia, to make up for the Gulf crisis shortfall, threatened to create an oil supply glut. As many as 8 large oil tankers with unsold cargos anchored off the European coast in November 1990.

Price increases stimulate technological innovation. An example is the energy-saving fluorescent light bulb (Stipp, 1990). The bulb cost about $15, screwed into standard sockets, and had about the same color and intensity of regular 60-watt bulbs, but it used only 15 watts of electricity. Moreover, it lasted 10 times longer. With greater sales volume, the price would come down to $10. If 25% of the power used for lighting in the United States came from fluorescent light bulbs instead of incandescents, the need for new capital-intensive power plants that burned conventional fuels or relied on nuclear power would decline. Many utilities, and more important, many of the public utility commissions that regulated them, accepted the idea of rewarding the utilities for marketing such efficiency-enhancing mechanisms instead of electricity. Boston Edison offered the fluorescent bulbs to customers for $3 a piece, sending employees door to door to install the bulbs to make sure that they would be used.

Innovative entrepreneurs could design and deliver a package of new technologies to industrial users (Emshwiller, 1990), but they had to be in close touch with customers. There were around 35 steps, for example, that could be taken to change industrial motors and their components, with savings of roughly half the energy the motors consumed. The payback came in about a year. But to design and carry out the changes, the entrepreneurs had to address many areas, including consumer education, selection and installation of equipment, financing, and maintenance. Producers of the innovations might have to offer a performance guarantee through an insurance company, assuring that if the savings were not realized they would absorb a percentage of the shortfall.

Conservation and natural gas were the best alternatives to petroleum, but the most abundant was coal. Proven coal reserves in the United States were large enough to last another three centuries at current consumption levels. This fuel, however, was dirty. Safety too was a matter of concern, especially with the mining of coal. There simply were few opportunities left for coal use; already 57% of the electricity produced in the United States came from coal-fired generating plants, whereas oil supplied only 5% of U.S. power. More electricity was generated from nuclear, natural gas, hydro, geothermal, and solar sources than from oil. Coal could replace gasoline as a vehicle fuel, but only to a limited extent and at a very high price. In South Africa, which could not rely on other nations to supply it with petroleum, conversion of coal for this purpose had been common for many years, but the process of making coal into gasoline was dirty and expensive and the South African government had to heavily subsidize it.

Canadian tar sands were another alternative. An estimated 300 billion barrels of oil were recoverable from the Athabasca region in northern and western Canada. Syncrude Canada Ltd., a partially owned subsidiary of Exxon, converted tar sands into 180,000 barrels of oil a day. Suncor, Inc., a unit of Sun Company of Philadelphia, made 60,000 barrels of oil a day from tar sands. Oil prices only had to remain substantially higher than $25 a barrel for these ventures to be commercially viable. Venezuela, too, was capable of producing a super-heavy crude from tar sands found in its Orinoco Belt. The product made in Venezuela was extremely dense, however, and without the addition of water, was difficult to transport.

Another alternative was oil shale (see the discussion in Chapter 6). The United States had proven reserves of 600 billion barrels of oil, equivalent to *all* of OPEC's proven reserves, but the costs of extracting usable oil from shale could run as high as $100 for the equivalent of a barrel of oil. The problem was that the extensive process of breaking down and crushing the rock that was necessary to capture the small residues of trapped oil was extremely expensive and environmentally damaging. An operating shale oil plant was very capital intensive and would require immense government subsidies. With vast government subsidies, Unocal's Parachute Creek plant only lowered costs to the equivalent of $40 a barrel of imported oil.

In the 1970s, the United States had turned to gasohol, a mixture of gasoline and grain alcohol (ethanol). The hope was that this product would expand the market for corn, reduce pollution, and lessen U.S. dependence on foreign oil. Adding ethanol to gasoline raises the octane level and causes the gasoline to burn more cleanly. In midwestern farm states (Minnesota, for example) gasohol sales peaked at nearly 33% of the market in 1985. The sale of gasohol has since declined to less 10% of the market. Rumors started that gasohol could destroy carburetor seals, hurt engine valves, and erode the paint from car surfaces. These charges were untrue, but price remained a problem: At about $1.50 a gallon, gasohol simply was not competitive with gasoline.

Another option was propane, a fuel already used in over 300,000 vehicles even without government subsidies. Very low in pollution, especially the ground-level pollution that plagues big cities, 85% of it is derived as a by-product from domestic oil and natural gas production. The remaining 15% comes from non-OPEC countries such as Canada and Mexico. Mostly used for heating, propane is a much neglected fuel for motor vehicles. It could propel up to 3.5% of the vehicles on U.S. roads with little difficulty. The problem is obtaining additional supplies.

Solar power also might play a role in reducing U.S. dependence on foreign energy supplies. Solar power comes in many forms (see the discussion of photovoltaic cells in Appendix 1). Rapid technological advances have reduced photovoltaic prices to where they are competitive in limited applications. Another solar option is trough-like collectors that can be used in very sunny climates to produce electricity. In southern California, these solar collectors have been successfully manufactured by Luz International Ltd., which produces nearly 90% of the world's solar-generated electricity. Nonetheless, the potential for replacing foreign petroleum is small, because the utilities in the sun-drenched regions of the Southwest, which would buy solar power, use little petroleum to generate electricity. The price for a kilowatt-hour of solar-generated power fell from 24 cents a decade ago to 8 cents in 1990. Another 2-cent-per-kilowatt-hour decline would make the price of solar-generated power competitive with other forms of electric generation.

Geothermal power also could play a role in reducing U.S. dependence. Unocal Corporation has reserves off the southern California coast that are the equivalent of 216 million barrels of oil. It plans to spend millions of dollars in the next few years exploring for additional geothermal energy off the coasts of California, the Philippines, and Indonesia. Geothermal power, though, has major limitations. Created only where the earth's crusts have established certain geologic conditions of heat, temperature, and pressure, this type of energy cannot be transported, but must be used near the spot from where it comes. Generating electricity with geothermal energy is very expensive, about 9.5 cents per kilowatt-hour for Unocal's Salton Sea facility, in contrast to 4.5 cents to 7.5 cents for electricity from more conventional sources.

A Tax on Energy

In sum, it seems clear that to further stimulate innovation and energy-saving behavior, a tax on energy use is needed (McCracken, 1990). Otherwise, none of the alternatives will be competitive with oil. A tax would make many of the alternatives more attractive. It would reduce the payback period for all types of conservation measures and would stimulate alternative production. The market, not the government, would choose which alternative to emphasize based on a host of factors of concern to users, including cost and convenience. But such a tax has not been something that either the Bush administration or Congress has been willing to consider. The Japanese in effect have such a tax and as a consequence are likely to continue to outperform the United States in conservation gains and technological breakthroughs. The contrasting, relatively low energy prices in the United States have many negative effects, including urban sprawl and the concentration of social problems in core city areas.

If the price of gasoline in the United States had risen just as fast as the other items on the Consumer Price Index in 1980s, by 1990 Americans would have been paying $2 a gallon for gasoline, which was much closer to what people in other countries were paying (McCracken, 1990). The higher price would have encouraged Americans to drive fewer miles in smaller cars and to take other energy-saving measures. Instead, the relatively low U.S. price for gasoline sent the exact opposite message.

2

Energy Economics

Trends in energy production and consumption from World War II to the Iraqi invasion of Kuwait are examined to illuminate patterns in energy trade, efficiency, and prices. This examination provides insight into the broader issue of whether energy scarcity is possible. Consistent with economic doctrine, a commodity in scarce supply becomes more expensive, which encourages conservation, the discovery of new supplies, and technological breakthroughs. These factors make it highly unlikely that the world can "run out" of a key resource like energy. But in the short term, unexpected supply interruptions and price instability can be extremely damaging and have negative effects on inflation, growth, and productivity as well as on other economic indicators, as will be shown in this chapter.

Energy Trends Since World War II

From 1949 to 1989, the world experienced three energy price epochs, one in which energy prices declined, one in which they rose, and one in which they fell again (Energy Information Administration, 1987, 1989). From 1949 to 1973, the composite real price per million Btu of the major fuels—crude oil, natural gas, and coal—declined 66%. From

1974 to 1981, this price rose 97%, and from 1981 to 1988, it declined again, this time by 40%. This volatility in world energy prices stemmed mainly from volatility in oil prices. Coal and natural gas prices were relatively stable, and unstable oil prices led companies and individuals to switch from oil when practicable. Electric utilities phased out many oil-fired power plants in the 1970s, using these plants only as backup capacity and replacing them with coal- and nuclear-generated power. In the transportation sector, alternatives to gasoline for propelling automobiles were not as feasible, but in the industrial sector, companies found many ways to move from a dependence on oil. Households too used less energy, but dispersed decision making at the household level as well as ownership problems—many people were renters—put a limit on the potential savings.

For most of the post-World War II period, energy consumption was closely tied to economic growth (Erol & Yu, 1988; Wang & Latham, 1989; Yu & Choi, 1985). From 1949 and 1973, consumption doubled and the U.S. economy grew at about same rate, but after 1973 energy use and economic growth did not run as closely in parallel. The U.S. economy grew less rapidly, and it used less energy to achieve growth. The mix of fuels changed. The United States moved from heavy oil and gas consumption toward increased reliance on electrical power. Oil and gas, 77% of total U.S. energy use in 1973, slipped to 66% by 1988. Even though electricity use rose, demand did not increase as rapidly as it did prior to 1973, when it grew at a rate of about 7% per year, which translated into a doubling of demand each decade. After 1973, growth in demand for electricity slowed to about 3% per year and utility planners canceled orders for many electric power plants.

U.S. petroleum imports followed the lead of unstable petroleum prices (Darmstadter, Landsberg, Morton, & Coda, 1983). With the oil price collapse of 1986, petroleum consumption grew because of more highway travel, stimulated by higher real disposable incomes and adverse weather conditions. With greater consumption, the capability of the strategic petroleum reserve to supply U.S. markets declined. In 1985, the reserve could supply U.S. oil markets for 115 days, but by 1988, the capability to supply these markets had dropped to 88 days. But even with greater demand and the decline in domestic reserves, prices went down in 1988 because of excess OPEC production.

After 1973, the oil-producing nations exploited relatively inelastic petroleum demand by raising prices (Alm & Weiner, 1984). By the early 1980s, the effects of the world's response were apparent (Tsai, 1989).

Conservation, fuel switching, and increased efficiency had inhibited demand, and the higher prices had stimulated new sources of production in non-OPEC countries. World demand for petroleum, 56 million barrels per day in 1973, dipped after the 1973 price hike, and then grew to 65 million barrels per day in 1979. After the 1979-1980 increases in prices, consumption again fell, dropping to 59 million barrels per day in 1983. At that point, lower demand and excess production (recall that there was a major world recession) further eroded prices, but as prices declined, consumption started to increase again. By 1986, it was 61 million barrels per day, with U.S. consumption 16 million barrels per day of the 35 million used by the OECD countries. Japan used 4 million barrels per day. Among non-OECD countries, the USSR was the biggest oil consumer, using 9 million barrels of oil a day.

The Debate About Energy Scarcity

What were the possibilities that the world would someday run out of petroleum? To answer this question it is necessary to delve into the economics of natural resources and the controversies that the literature in this area has engendered (Simon, 1981; Smith, 1979). Economists in the Malthusian mold always forecast ultimate doom because of resource scarcity, but the United States was a richly endowed country. By any standard, until the mid-1900s resources were plentiful. Concern for the adequacy of resources to sustain economic growth made little sense. Even with a growing population, economists believed that technological advances would assure adequate supplies. As time progressed, low-grade resources simply would take the place of high-grade resources (Smith, 1979). The replacement of one type of resource by another would be accompanied by technological changes that would ease the transition. Such cycles in resource use were common. They could be seen in the historical experience of minerals such as iron ore. Once very abundant and easily processed, iron ore became less abundant and what remained was less easily processed; nonetheless, its price had not increased in real terms and noticeable shortages in supply had not taken place.

The oil embargo of 1973 rekindled controversy about whether the process actually would work as economists predicted. The dominant view was that any supply problem, should it exist, was distant. Vast potential new supplies of high-grade oil and natural gas were still available. Knowledge of the physical composition of the earth's crust was limited, as was knowledge of the location, amount, and quality of the available energy deposits. At current usage rates, low-grade reserves of coal, tar sands, and shale extended supplies hundreds of years into the future. Nonetheless, there were questions: the extent to which the low-grade stocks could be easily extracted and the extent to which they could be effectively converted to oil substitutes, given their impurities. Processing costs for the low-grade resources were likely to be quite high. Resource-augmenting technical progress would be needed to lower extraction and processing costs and to increase efficiencies in use, so that existing supplies would extend further into the future. Finally, a different type of technical progress might be necessary to yield new substances or processes that would completely alter the way energy was made and used. Technology also could play a role not simply in expanding the existing stock of energy that would be used in a conventional manner, but in radically altering the forms and means (e.g., an electric car) of energy production and use. But would this technological progress be forthcoming (Smith & Krutilla, 1979)?

For economists who adhered to the neoclassical tradition, running out of a vital natural resource was impossible (Stiglitz, 1979). A natural resource was like the other factors of production, and all production factors—labor, capital, and resources—could be substituted for each other. Other economists held that the extensive adjustments implied by factor substitutions violated physical laws (Daly, 1979). These economists challenged the realism of an argument that the world could survive without natural resources. According to these economists, it was not possible to indefinitely convert so-called low-entropy energy resources to their higher-entropy forms. These economists were far from the mainstream, but attracted attention during the anxious 1970s.

Even economists operating within a more conventional framework admitted that the substitution of capital and labor for natural resources might not take place smoothly and the process might not occur indefinitely. An issue of great importance was the time frame of the substitution. Neoclassical economists had not worked out the detailed timing of how the transition to a new resource regime would take place. Moreover, they were likely to admit that without some input of natural resources, even if only an infinitesimal amount, production could not take place. The neoclassical framework required some natural resources for production, but a small input might be all that was needed if it could be compensated for with a sufficiently large input of capital.

Price was not the only factor that stimulated resource substitution, however. Broad historical forces were at work, forces such as the stage of economic growth and the associated material and natural resource use. Even without changes in energy prices, the U.S. economy and the economy of other industrialized nations were undergoing a transformation toward less intensive energy and materials use. With this shift from processing basic materials toward the production of increasingly refined and complex goods (e.g., computer chips and electric board circuits) that required less energy and material input (Williams & Larson, 1987), future industrial energy requirements would be lower than projected regardless of energy prices. The change was taking place because rapidly growing and important sectors of the economy were not energy intensive. The typical economy exhibited the following pattern of growth: intensity of resource use with expanding per capita GNP in the early stages, plateauing in later stages, and decline with maturity.

Market Imperfections

Economists posited a smooth transition to less abundant resources provided that markets functioned properly (i.e., price signals were appropriate and people responded to them by making rational self-interested choices). But there are challenges to the smooth functioning of markets. As air, water, and other environmental amenities lack owner or price, developers of new energy resources use them without paying for them and thereby pass the actual costs on to society. Unless government attaches a price to the environmental degradation to make up for the market failing to do so, the development of these resources would proceed without precautions to limit the environmental harm. A related issue was that as dependence on specific natural resources decreased, some of the materials that took their place were likely to be synthetic compounds that bore almost no relation to materials occurring in nature. They too might become the source of significant and pervasive environmental harm.

It was not only market imperfections that had to be considered. Government imperfections played a role. In the environmental area, for instance, the government had to find a mechanism to appropriately charge for environmental harm. Economists favored a pollution tax or charge system: For each ton of pollutant emitted the polluter had to pay the tax or charge. Avoiding payment would be an incentive to pollute less. Rather than the government dictating how to eliminate discharges, polluters would see that it was in their interest to make cost-saving innovations. The government, however, had to decide what the price for pollution would be, and this was no easy matter. In any event, the government continued to rely on regulation, not on pricing pollution harms.

The inclination on the part of the government to regulate rather than to rely on market forces had other manifestations. For instance, in the 1970s the U.S. government intervened in energy markets to keep prices of natural gas and petroleum artificially low when it would have better to allow them to rise to their market-clearing levels (Solo, 1987). Artificially low prices failed to provide producers with an incentive to explore for new supplies and failed to provide consumers with an incentive to conserve; this led to demand greater than supply and contributed to the long lines at gas stations. The history of inappropriate government intervention was an old one. The Eisenhower administration introduced quotas on foreign imports of petroleum products to maintain domestic supplies and assure national security. Exactly the opposite was achieved: Without imports, domestic supplies were rapidly depleted and the United States became heavily dependent on foreign imports.

Most economists, however, admitted that government had a role in guaranteeing high enough prices to stimulate R&D. Without that incentive, the immediate effect of technological change was to lower prices, thus making it counterproductive to make the discovery in the first place. Breakthroughs might have social benefits that could not be entirely captured by the party responsible if, for example, society enjoyed more jobs and new business development for which the discoverer was not adequately compensated (Solo, 1987, p. 146).

Markets had another defect—their inability to adequately reflect future interests. Motivated by the sovereignty of present-day consumers, they did not deal effectively with the future. Economists countered that this problem was not significant. Many uncertainties existed, and markets were the best way to deal with them, because markets systematically aggregated individual beliefs, and individuals acting in their own best interests had the incentive to discover systematic errors. An inability to accurately foresee the future, in any event, was not critical: If the present generation left few resources, future generations would have a higher level of technology and more capital. Therefore, they would be better off and thus it might be in their interests for present generations to consume more rather than less. Other economists questioned the dogma that technology could always substitute new resources for old without limit.

Unexpected Price Shocks

In the long run, energy availability depended upon the existence of low-grade energy resources; labor, capital, and natural resource substitution; the external effects of these substitutions; the functioning of futures markets; and government interventions. And in the long run, there was evidence of structural change in the United States and the world economy shifting from more intensive toward less intensive energy use. In the long run, energy scarcity might not be an important problem, and in the short term, absent major wars or other events to disrupt energy shipments, shortages were not likely to occur (Pindyck, 1979). A country should be able to import the energy it wanted by offering a high enough price. If governments did not attempt to keep fuel price below market-clearing levels, the energy should be readily available to consumers who could afford it. The real problem in the short term was unexpected price shocks—large-scale, unanticipated increases in the prices of energy.

After the multinational oil corporations (e.g., Exxon, Mobil, Shell) lost ownership of crude oil to the oil-producing states, the producing states controlled production levels and prices. They restricted the role of the multinationals to transportation and downstream refining. Actions by them brought on worldwide energy crises: the near quadrupling of oil prices that followed the Arab-Israeli War (from $3.50 a barrel in 1973 to $13.50 a barrel in 1974) and the near tripling of oil prices that followed the Iran-Iraq War (from $13.50 a barrel in 1979 to $34.50 a barrel in 1980). With the first of these price shocks, inflation rates rose from an already high 8% in the world's major industrialized countries (except for Switzerland) to double-digit levels (Tsai, 1989). Economic growth in the industrialized countries slumped from an average annual rate of 4.9% in 1965-1973 to 2.7% in 1973-1979. Similar effects occurred after the second price shock.

Price shocks caused more domestic resources to be traded for each unit of energy, with a loss in consumer purchasing power. The 1974 increase in oil prices meant a transfer of about 2% of GDP from the developed countries to the oil-exporting countries (Tsai, 1989). The deterioration in terms of trade meant lost real income for the oil-importing countries with less real total national income being available for domestic consumption and investment. No economic policy could offset this decline in wages, profits, and consumption, but fiscal and monetary policies, which affected the inflation rate and national investment, influenced how economies absorbed the damage and how well they rebounded from it. The extent of the damage, in turn, depended on the share of a country's GNP in energy and the degree to which consumers were willing to change habits to reduce energy use (Pindyck, 1979).

Energy use fell immediately after price increases, but replacing durable capital goods took time. To achieve long-run gains, the durable capital goods had to be replaced. Estimates of the impact of the 1973-1974 price shock on U.S. economic growth were a decline of about 3% to 5.5% in GNP in 1975 (Huntington, 1985). For 1979-1980, estimates were of a 2% to 4% decline in GNP. When real wages did not fall to the level demanded by higher energy prices, employers refused to hire. Unemployment grew. In Europe, it was 9% to 11% during the 1970s and in the United States 6% to 7%. The oil price shocks produced immediate short-term bursts of inflation, which considerably slowed by the third year.

Policymakers had trouble dealing with the simultaneous high unemployment and high inflation (Bohi, 1989). The tendency was for macroeconomic policies during the 1970s to have a stop-and-go character, as policymakers waffled over which problem, inflation or unemployment, to tackle. They reduced price pressures via restrictive policies that slowed economic growth and added to unemployment; and then they tried to protect jobs by pursuing policies that added to inflation. The 1979-1980 price shock and double-digit U.S. inflation brought a return to restrictive policies. The first priority became the fight against inflation, but the restrictive policies contributed to the strong recession the U.S. economy experienced in 1979-1982 (Pindyck & Rotemberg, 1984).

The mix of durable capital goods in the U.S. economy changed with adjustments to higher prices. The incentive was to shift away from the use of capital and energy toward labor-intensive production. This shift may have contributed to a decline in productivity, which only made recessionary conditions worse. The service sector, which was less capital intensive and required less energy, grew. But it was also more resistant than the industrial sector to productivity improvement.

Prior to 1973, the industrial countries carried a balance of payment surplus on current accounts of about $13 billion, the developing countries had a corresponding deficit, and the industrialized countries provided the developing countries with aid and capital. In 1974, the current accounts deficit of the industrial countries exceeded $23 billion, and the oil-exporting countries had a massive foreign exchange surplus, which expanded from $6 billion in 1973 to more than $60 billion in 1974. By 1980, the cumulative surplus of the oil-exporting nations was about $107 billion. The oil-exporting countries had two options: They could use the increase in revenues to import additional goods or they could acquire assets in other parts of the world. When the exporting countries spent 40% to 45% of their additional oil revenues on imports, they stimulated the world economy; for 1973-1978, their average spending for imports was almost 55%, indicating a positive effect on world economic growth. After the second oil shock, these countries' spending for imports was lower, only 5% in 1979 compared to 30% in 1974, and only 24% in 1980 compared to 49% in 1975. The effect on world economic growth was negative, and the lack of spending contributed to the worldwide recession that followed the 1979-1980 price hike.

Ultimately, the world economy adjusted to higher energy prices. Among other factors, declining economic growth affected energy use. Conservation, alternative energy use, and the rise in non-OPEC oil production drove down the price of oil. By 1986, crude oil prices had declined to about $12 a barrel from a high of $40 (Shaaf, 1985). The very fabric of OPEC began to unravel during the 1979-1982 world economic recession as OPEC nations, hungry for oil revenues, sold capacity in excess of OPEC quotas on the spot market (see Chapter 4). The Soviet Union's vast energy reserves also started to enter Western markets via shipments of natural gas to Europe. The relative decline in world energy prices dampened inflation and contributed to world economic growth.

As the profits of the major oil-producing companies and states declined, there were cutbacks in exploration, which could mean shortages in the future. For oil-exporting nations like Mexico and Nigeria, the reduction in oil revenues meant possible default on a large national debt. (Mexico's debt exceeded $100 billion and Nigeria's was nearly $20 billion.) For the Soviet Union, the reduction in oil prices put greater pressure on an economy already burdened by the heightened expectations of *perestroika*. For the oil-rich regions in the southwestern United States, the reduction in oil prices meant that complete economic recovery receded far into the future. For Iran and Iraq, it meant problems in rebuilding their war-torn economies. Some believed that oil prices had plunged too far and they argued that $15 a barrel was a desirable floor, whereas others maintained that the real price of energy in current dollars had averaged only $12 a barrel throughout the 20th century (1901-1985) and should remain at that level.

Impacts on World Economic Growth

Energy use had been ubiquitous in history pervading nearly every aspect of life (Schurr, 1987). Coal contributed to the development of the iron and steel industry, railways, and factory mechanization. Electrification and motorized transport contributed to 20th century economic growth. Some analysts proposed a doctrine of inseparability, meaning that the connection between growth and consumption could not be broken. Less energy use signified a reduction in real wealth. Because ample energy supplies were available, conservation, in any event, was not needed. The opposing view was that less energy use would not damage the economy. Consumption to support a given level of economic activity could be changed. Per capita consumption in the United States was substantially higher than in other industrialized nations, and the U.S. energy/output ratio far exceeded that of countries such as France, West Germany, and Sweden, whose per capita income and output were roughly similar.

The explanations for the differences in energy consumption in different nations were complex, including different pricing policies, the extent to which the countries were import independent, their product mix, and the state of their technology. The composition of GNP, exchange rates, climate, and geography also played a role, as did environmental, demographic, and sociological factors. Sweden and Canada had similar living standards and climate, but energy consumption in Canada was about twice what it was in Sweden. The Eastern bloc countries had much higher energy consumption rates per unit of GNP than Western European countries. Underdeveloped countries had low energy to GNP ratios, but as they developed, their energy to GNP ratios grew. When the economic growth rates of developed countries slackened, their energy to GNP ratios tended to fall.

Evidence suggested a strong relationship between economic growth rates and energy consumption in the United States. From 1850 to 1975 there was a positive correlation between per capita energy consumption and per capita GNP (Schurr, 1987). Until 1973, average annual growth rates of energy consumption and GNP in the United States were virtually identical—3.2% and 3.3%, respectively (Darmstadter, Landsberg, Morton, & Coda, 1983). But from 1888 to 1920, energy consumption increased 1.5 times faster than GNP. Heavy energy consumption was associated with the fast growth rate of manufacturing relative to agriculture. From 1920 to 1960 energy consumption expanded slower than GNP, only 0.75 times the economic growth rate. The decline was due to factors such as electrification, which enhanced the efficiency of factory operations.

Cross-sectional and international studies corroborated the findings of a close relationship between energy consumption and economic development. For OECD countries as a whole, the 1960-1973 period saw a 1% increase in energy usage associated with 1% increase in GDP; however, between 1973 and 1981, when GDP grew at average rate of 2.3% annually, consumption of total primary energy grew by only .2% annually. This decline in energy intensity reflects structural changes in the use of energy, responses to energy policies and prices, and effects of the business cycle. High energy prices and conservation helped break the link between economic growth and energy consumption (Tsai, 1989).

The feedback effects between energy and the economy were complex. Energy had an impact on the economy and in turn was affected by it. Energy consumption was both a necessary condition for growth and a consequence of it. Energy consumption also affected productivity. The conventional wisdom was that the oil price shocks contributed to the slowdowns in productivity growth in the United States and the world in the 1970s (Berndt & Wood, 1987). But energy may have played no role, as there were many explanations for this slowdown and economists could not agree on a single cause. Among the possibilities were:

1. Energy conservation was the chief culprit for the productivity slowdown.
2. Energy could not be the cause given its small share in total production costs.
3. The slowdown was caused by idle and uncooperative workers.
4. The slowdown was directly related to monetary and fiscal policies and the effect of energy price shocks was indirect.
5. Decreased investment rates in plant and equipment and in R&D were at fault.
6. The slowdown was affected by capital goods, which became obsolete because they no longer were energy efficient.
7. The slowdown was affected by the substitution of labor for energy, which was induced by higher energy prices.

Energy efficiency gains required investment in new capital plant and equipment. Much post-1973 investment had energy efficiency as one of its chief goals. An attempt was made to replace the energy-inefficient capital with more energy-efficient designs. The capital investment that came on line in 1978-1981 yielded energy efficiency, but perhaps at the expense of worker productivity. Rising labor productivity depended upon the substitution of energy and machines for labor. Energy that was cheap and abundant and available in flexible forms, like petroleum, natural gas, and electricity, stimulated discovery, development, and use of new processes, equipment, and systems of production. It opened up new locational possibilities and quickened the speed of technical change. But in the 1970s energy suddenly became expensive and failed to breed the same type of productivity enhancement via technological innovation that occurred previously. High energy prices meant more labor intensity and declines in labor productivity (the service sector grew) with reductions in energy use.

To conclude, the energy shocks of the 1970s contributed to the stagflation that was the dominant feature of the world economy in the 1970s. Large increases in the price of imported oil and in the costs of domestic energy affected the general price level. Real disposable income and consumer wealth went down, depressing consumption expenditure and aggregate demand. The value lost in sectors of the economy that contracted outpaced the value gained in sectors that expanded, making GNP less than it otherwise would have been. The wealth transfers went from the users to the owners of energy resources and from the importing to the exporting countries. The income that exporting countries earned was not injected back into the economy in the form of imports at a rate high enough to compensate for the losses. The effect was the same as that of an excise tax, after which the government fails to return resources to the economy as transfers or additional expenditures. Over the long term, however, the nations of the world adjusted to the new conditions. They made changes in capital stock and technology. They replaced obsolete plant and equipment with energy-efficient stock. In the process, they became less dependent on foreign energy. But they had to divert resources from other uses that might, under different circumstances, have been more productively deployed. Thus, the productivity of the world economy and its potential to grow declined.

3

U.S. Government Policies

This chapter starts on a normative note with a brief sketch of the economic theory of what governments *should* do with regard to energy markets. Then follows a historical overview of what the U.S. government *actually* did, with a review of U.S. government policies prior to 1973, during the onset of the first energy crisis, and through the second energy crisis of 1979 (Levine, 1985; Schwartz, 1987). In this chapter I concentrate on three types of policies that the U.S. government pursued during this period—conservation, R&D programs, and energy price decontrol—and assess the effectiveness of these policies. To be sure, by the mid-1980s imports had declined, but to what extent were the policies that the U.S. government carried out responsible for this outcome? I argue here that because the policies worked at cross-purposes (they both stimulated and suppressed demand), their impact was substantially diluted. The intent of the government policies was to prevent sudden price increases from inflicting dramatic losses on energy consumers and producers. The complex system of compensatory intervention the government used to cushion these groups from the impact of higher oil prices, as is shown in this chapter, failed to make major headway in changing patterns of energy use and reducing U.S. dependence on foreign oil (Tugwell, 1988).

Theory and Practice

Economists generally prefer decentralized decision making by consumers in the marketplace to the centralized control of the government. This preference is based not only on the efficiency advantages of markets but also on their encouragement of economic and technological progress, a rising standard of living, social mobility, and political freedom (Friedman & Friedman, 1980). One of the main proofs that markets outperform government comes from the experience of the newly industrialized economies of Asia, which have done so much better than the state-centered economies of Eastern Europe and the Soviet Union. Nonetheless, almost all economists admit that markets are not perfect and that they have certain defects or shortcomings that should be corrected by government action. For instance, economic efficiency requires that there be competitive factor and product markets; that is, there must be no obstacles to the free entry of new market participants and full market knowledge by existing producers and consumers. These conditions are rarely met fully by markets. Another defect of markets is that they may not adequately protect future rights and interests. Government intervention may be justified because private and public perspectives on the valuation of the present and future differ (see Chapter 2). Further, economists admit that even if markets operate according to theory, they do not provide those types of public goods, the need for which is felt collectively rather than individually.

Private market activities create so-called spillovers or externalities. A positive spillover or externality exists when a producer cannot appropriate all the benefits of the activities it has undertaken. An example would be research and development that yields benefits to society (e.g., employment in subsidiary industries) that the producer cannot capture. Here the producer's incentive is to underinvest in the activity unless government subsidizes it. With positive externalities, too little of the good in question is produced. With negative ones, too much is made. Negative externalities like air pollution occur when the producer cannot be charged all the costs. Because the external costs do not enter into the calculations the producer makes, the producer manufactures more of the good than is socially beneficial. With both positive and negative externalities, market outcomes need correction to be efficient.

Many, but not all, economists accept that two additional market defects exist. To correct for the first, the apparent instabilities in the business cycle, the government can implement a variety of fiscal and monetary policies. The government can also correct for the second, unequal outcomes of market processes by, for example, redistributing income via the tax code or inheritance laws.

These broad principles of market defects have to be applied to energy markets. Markets maximize efficiency, with government intervention being necessary only under special conditions, such as when energy markets are not perfectly competitive and monopoly power yields inadequate production and excessive prices. The OPEC cartel, formed in the late 1960s by the governments of the oil-producing states (who are beyond the reach of U.S. antitrust regulations), has as its purpose to use its monopoly power to limit production and raise energy prices. The existence of a cartel like OPEC may justify some type of government intervention to break the cartel. Demand reduction and developing alternative sources of supply reduce the power of the cartel, but how the governments of the world should intervene to bring about these results is unclear.

Energy production and use can also generate external costs and benefits that call for government correction. Pollution exemplifies an external cost of energy development activities that requires government intervention. Research and development expenses may not be taken on by private-sector companies in a way that is socially optimal without government involvement. Further, market prices may not adequately signal the possible depletion of an exhaustible resource like petroleum or fully take into account the national security costs of acquiring this resource. These factors too may require government attention. Finally, many economists believe that governments should intervene if energy markets fail to achieve equity, but this view is controversial.

In all of these instances where a rationale exists for government involvement, it does not necessarily follow from the rationale that the government is capable of effectively correcting the defect. Markets are not perfect, but governments too have shortcomings, and their ability to correct market imperfections is limited. In each instance of a market defect, it is necessary to weigh whether the proposed government action would improve the situation.

The reality of government intervention in energy markets does not match the theory articulated by economists. Government policies are crafted not by economists but by politicians. In the deliberations that determine political outcomes, it is not the barter system of the market that is most influential but the Constitutional system of checks and balances instituted by the founders of the nation. The founders imagined a large country with diverse interests. Fearful of powerful majorities, they tried to create a system where no faction could dominate. The participants in political controversies, therefore, are wide ranging and diverse, including citizens, interest groups, corporations, trade associations, environmental organizations, federal bureaucrats, and the media. Different professional groups—scientists, physicians, engineers, lawyers—provide expert opinion. Sages, seers, and pundits testify in front of congressional committees, appear on talk shows, and write newspaper columns. Policy is affected by factual information, theory, beliefs, values, attitudes, conjectures, statistics, and anecdotes. The history of U.S. energy policies is no orderly process of deliberation based on abstract economic principles (McKie, 1984).

The twists and turns in the development of U.S. energy policies are complex. Before 1970, a state agency, the Texas Railroad Commission, effectively controlled U.S. petroleum output (most U.S. oil came from Texas) through prorationing regulations that provided multiple owners with the rights to underground pools. The federal government provided tax breaks in the form of intangible drilling expenses and gave the oil companies a depletion allowance. The program in place from 1959 to 1973, which limited oil imports, protected domestic producers from cheap foreign oil. With the ostensible purpose of maintaining national security, this policy contributed to the depletion of domestic reserves.

Policies for the natural gas industry had different objectives but similar results: depletion rather than preservation of reserves. Natural gas was discovered during the drilling for oil. Initially, it was flared and burned because no pipeline system existed to transport it to markets. The purpose of the laws passed by Congress to regulate natural gas prices was to keep prices high enough to justify the large capital investment needed to construct a pipeline system. The Natural Gas Act of 1938 gave the Federal Power Commission (FPC) the right to control prices and limit any new pipelines from entering the market. The Supreme Court (in the 1954 Phillips decision) extended price controls to field production. Low prices then stimulated widespread adoption, and natural gas replaced coal for home heating and numerous industrial uses. For cities that had suffered from the soot and dirt of coal, conversion to natural gas was a great benefit. But the prices the FPC set for natural gas were not high enough to induce conservation or exploration; the natural gas industry failed to replace the gas as it was used, and proven reserves declined.

The government promoted electricity use through rural electrification and other programs. As the real costs of generating and distributing electricity declined, the utilities enjoyed the advantages of rate regulation by public utility commissions. A protected monopoly with a guaranteed rate of return made the risk of investment low. Because the formula for determining utility revenue was based on the amount of investment, the tendency was to "gold-plate" systems by overinvesting in plant and equipment. Overcapitalization took a special form in government subsidies to the nuclear power industry. Under the supervision of the congressional Joint Committee on Atomic Energy, the Atomic Energy Commission (AEC) promoted "peaceful uses of the atom." Nuclear power promised a future in which electricity from nuclear power plants "would be too cheap to meter" (see Chapter 7). Congress passed the 1957 Price Anderson Act, which limited the liability of each nuclear plant to $560 million in case of an accident provided it conformed to the safety standards set by the government. The government encouraged the development of reprocessing facilities for spent fuel and tried to assure the industry that it would find ways to dispose of long-lived nuclear waste.

Prior to the 1973 Arab oil embargo, separate forms of government intervention evolved to cover different kinds of energy. These energy policies had a common denominator: to keep prices low and consumption high. Given the close connection between energy consumption and economic growth that prevailed at the time, these goals were not unreasonable. Unfortunately, the unintended consequence was more rapid depletion. In 1970 oil production in the United States peaked and started to decline. Natural gas production peaked in 1973 and has dropped since. The United States started to import oil at a rate of about 6 million barrels of oil per day. It no longer had the technical capacity to achieve self-sufficiency (Schurr, 1979; U.S. Congress, Senate Committee on Energy and Natural Resources, 1987a). President Nixon took note of these changes prior to the Yom Kippur War.

The Oil Embargo: The Government Responds

Coinciding with the Yom Kippur War, the Arab petroleum-exporting countries imposed an embargo that quadrupled prices. The U.S. government had no choice but to respond in dramatic fashion, as the situation aroused intense fears among the U.S. people and created strong political pressures (see Table 3.1). The Emergency Petroleum Allocation Act that

Table 3.1 The Evolution of Federal Energy Policy After the 1973 Arab Oil Embargo

1973	The Emergency Petroleum Allocation Act
1974	Project Independence Federal Non-nuclear Research and Development Act Energy Supply and Coordination Act
1975	Energy Policy and Conservation Act
1977	Creation of Department of Energy (DOE) Federal Mine Safety and Health Amendments Act Clean Air Amendments Surface Mining Control and Reclamation Act (SMCR)
1978	Power Plant and Industrial Fuel Use Act Natural Gas Policy Act (NGPA) Public Utilities Regulatory Policy Act (PURPA) Gas Guzzler Tax Building Energy Performance Standards
1980	Decontrol of petroleum prices

Congress passed in 1973 gave the federal government the right to allocate fuel in a time of shortage (MacAvoy, 1983). To deal with the mounting inflation that existed prior to the embargo, the Cost of Living Council, which had been created in the White House, established wage and price guidelines and controlled oil prices. The Emergency Petroleum Allocation Act 1973 extended the existing oil price controls. The popular belief was that the oil companies were responsible for the higher prices that accompanied the embargo, and the public had to be protected both from the predatory practices of the industry and from the windfall profits it was earning. For producers operating under these price restrictions, the incentive was to withhold oil from the market. The Emergency Petroleum Allocation Act 1973 also mandated an entitlements plan, intended to equalize input prices among refiners, but small refiners, generally lacking access to domestic crude, were disproportionately favored. Oil producers were reluctant to release cheap domestic crude priced below market levels. Finally, the government sought to increase the inventories of fuel oil at the expense of gasoline and directly withheld fuel oil from the market to ensure heating oil supplies for the winter.

Thus, the 1973-1974 supply interruptions led to shortages, long lines at gas pumps in many sections of country, and intense public irritation, but these spot shortages were as much due to government allocations and price controls and interferences with marketing procedures as to a basic lack of supply. Additional postcrisis responses lasted for a number of years. In 1974, President Ford announced Project Independence, intended to completely eliminate U.S. dependence on foreign imports. The United States set up an emergency petroleum reserve and agreed to adhere to international agreements for allocating oil. The government policies, though, were not guided by a consistent or logically connected set of ends; rather they yielded a series of energy "czars" and reorganizations. The Federal Energy Office (FEO) came into being to administer price controls. Congress passed the Federal Nonnculear Research and Development Act of 1974 to focus government efforts on nonnuclear research. AEC research programs were incorporated into the newly created Energy Research and Development Administration (ERDA), and the Nuclear Regulatory Commission (NRC) took over AEC regulatory responsibilities. The theory behind the reorganization was to separate the activities of promotion and development from the activities of regulation. In another action in 1974, the temporary Federal Energy Office that had been set up in the White House became the permanent Federal Energy Administration (FEA), signifying its growing importance in the federal government. New programs in solar energy and energy conservation started, and the coal programs in the Department of the Interior (DOI) grew in size. State efforts intensified as states like California developed their own independent forecasting capabilities and conservation regulations.

Finally, in 1977 Congress approved the cabinet-level creation of the Department of Energy (DOE). DOE incorporated all the activities of ERDA. The FPC lost its independent status and was replaced by the Federal Energy Regulatory Commission (FERC), which also was brought into DOE. DOE immediately became enmeshed in controversies about its objectives and managerial capabilities. Its success was defined by barrels per day of domestic oil delivered, but it was incapable of producing oil by itself. The legislation it was supposed to carry out ultimately extended to virtually all energy supply and conservation technologies and included many programs to minimize the impacts of fast-changing energy prices on special groups such as low-income persons. Incentives went to new technologies on the grounds that government investment would speed their entry into the marketplace. DOE had a series of direct and indirect policy approaches at its disposal, designed to goad, urge, coerce, and prod the energy industry and the commercial, industrial, and residential sectors of the economy to make changes. The net impact, though, was probably to increase economic uncertainty. The many programs DOE administered made it difficult for individuals and businesses, who had to commit resources for the long term, to forecast what the payback would be. Changes in government policies along with those taking place in the marketplace made it difficult to plan. The rationales for programs dissipated, and as they became irrelevant they were discontinued. Investments that had been made based on the assumption of continuing government support lost their value. The Reagan administration went so far as to propose abolishing DOE, but Congress supported the department and would not allow the administration to carry out this plan. The battle over DOE's future led to disarray and demoralization in many areas, particularly conservation and renewable energy, the programs the Reagan administration disliked the most. Shortly after Reagan became president, many DOE programs were abolished, although DOE continued in reduced form.

Clashes between energy and environmental objectives were common. A leading example was the Trans Alaska Pipeline. In 1973 Congress overruled environmentalists' objections and allowed major oil companies to continue this project. Congress also opened the Alaskan North Slope to keep U.S. oil production going. In addition, the federal government pressured facilities to convert to coal regardless of the environmental consequences. The Energy Supply and Coordination Act of 1974 encouraged utilities to switch from oil and gas to coal and suspended air pollution requirements. When feasible, power plants built after 1974 were supposed to have coal-burning capacity. The Power Plant and Industrial Fuel Use Act of 1978 prohibited construction of electric power plants and major industrial fuel-burning installations that used gas or oil as a primary energy source except when alternative fuels were unavailable. The 1980 Carter coal commission report recommended government controls, incentives, and regulations to increase the use of coal and substitute it for imported oil.

The role that coal played in national energy policy was complex. At times it was viewed as an abundant fuel resource readily available as a substitute for other forms of energy. At times its role was limited to a possible alternative in the transition from exhaustible (oil) to renewable (solar) energy, and at times its importance was magnified as the source of almost limitless synthetic substitutes for petroleum-based products, thus playing a useful geopolitical role that offset the strategic dependence of the United States on foreign sources. None of these views of coal policy were consistently pursued, however, as periods of neglect followed bursts of promotional activity. Safety, health, and environmental concerns grew, diminishing the potential of coal for filling vital energy needs. Regulations increased and became more detailed and complex under the Federal Mine Safety and Health Amendments Act of 1977, which created the Black Lung Disability Trust Fund. The EPA under the Clean Air Act limited the amount of sulfur oxides burned in new power plants. Utilities either had to use low-sulfur coal or install scrubbers. EPA regulations prohibited significant deterioration of air quality in areas meeting its standards. The 1977 Clean Air Amendments required all new coal facilities to install scrubbers using best available control technology (BACT). This measure, designed to help preserve markets for high-sulfur coal, raised the costs of coal-based power considerably. The Surface Mining Control and Reclamation Act of 1977 held back the development of strip mines, especially in the West, by requiring the restoration of land to uses as good as those before mining began. The looming issues of the 1980s—acid rain and the greenhouse effect—also were to undermine the use of coal.

Conservation

From an environmental point of view, conservation was the best alternative to imported oil (Nivola, 1986). The Energy Policy and Conservation Act of 1975 launched numerous conservation programs including mandatory fuel economy for autos to achieve better fleet average fuel efficiency for new vehicles between 1978 and 1985 and building energy performance standards (BEPS) for new structures. After the 1979 supply shock the government even tried to discourage the "frivolous" consumption of petroleum on Sundays by prohibiting the sale of gasoline on that day.

Mandatory fuel economy standards aimed to increase fleet fuel efficiency averages from 18 mpg in 1978 to 27.5 mpg by 1985. The auto industry, however, only supported voluntary guidelines. It claimed the 1985 goal was unattainable and that it would be too costly for consumers. The Department of Transportation (DOT) argued that the standard was cost-effective in that consumers would recover the higher auto prices in reduced fuel expenditures. In 1978, Congress passed the so-called Gas Guzzler Tax, which imposed a punitive tax on new cars whose fuel economy was far below average standards.

Buildings used a third of the energy consumed in the United States. Analyses indicated substantial potential for cost-effective reduction. DOE tried to establish standards that would minimize the life cycle costs of energy, but the standards never presented a clear and simple description of what the government intended. Builders had substantial discretion to decide what to do. The housing industry was in a serious slump in the early 1980s (30% of the industry went out of business), and it complained vociferously to Congress. Congress transformed BEPS into a voluntary program, and the mandatory provisions only affected federal buildings. The automobile companies met the goal of 27.5 mpg fleet fuel efficiency standards, but the building industry had no goal to meet. After 1980, the Reagan administration cut back on all conservation efforts.

R&D

Government R&D programs were supposed to diversify the emphasis away from nuclear power. Large-scale demonstration projects were started in numerous areas, including projects to convert coal and solid wastes into liquid and gaseous fuels; to extract and process oil shale and tar sands; to develop a viable breeder reactor that would ensure a virtually inexhaustible source of uranium for electricity; and to provide solar energy for space heating, industrial process heat, and electricity. Basic problems, however, could not be solved in the time available, and the achievements of most of the demonstration projects were disappointing. At the same time, many important minor advances were made, including advances in commercializing cost-effective energy-conserving end-use technologies such as energy-efficient lighting systems, improved heat pumps, and better designed heating systems. Research successes also were achieved in the environmental, safety, and health areas, with advances in the understanding of nuclear power safety, indoor air pollution, and the problems of fossil fuel conversion. Promise existed with regard to new materials, motor technologies, and super-insulated homes.

Geller (1987) analyzed seven cases of energy-conserving innovations traceable to federal R&D programs. The researchers estimated that the original federal investments totalled $16 million and resulted in eventual savings equivalent to $68 billion. Federal investments were concentrated in areas where the incentives for and availability of private investment were severely limited or nonexistent; participation was justified on the grounds that the advances would have been slowed by industry fragmentation and the noncapturability or public-good nature of the basic research.

A notable success was the solid state electronic ballast for fluorescent lights, developed at the Lawrence Berkeley Laboratory under the direction of a research scientist named Sam Berman (Jewell, Selkowitz, & Verderber, 1980). The government first worked with entrepreneurial firms on this project, granting funding to conduct the research that large firms would not pursue on their own and small firms by themselves could not afford. The entrepreneurial firms helped develop the early prototypes for the solid state ballasts. Foreign companies began producing ballasts in 1980, and a dozen small U.S. manufacturers struggled along with the foreign firms to establish a market and improve the product. By 1984, GE and GTE announced that they would sell lamps designed to be operated with the special energy-saving ballasts, and in 1985 GE as well as Universal Manufacturing started to sell the ballasts.

In the private sector as well, many projects succeeded, but many failed to work as expected or were slow in achieving commercial acceptance. After 1980, the Reagan administration brought about rapid changes in research priorities. The conservation and solar research budgets were nearly eliminated. Fossil energy research also was cut back substantially. Increases came in basic research, high energy physics, and defense-related work, but not in energy.

Decontrol

A different approach to expanding energy supply and reducing demand was to end regulation and work through the price system (MacAvoy, 1983; McKie, 1984). Most economists were very critical of the complex system of energy price regulations the government had evolved and the other programs it was supporting. The economists preferred to rely on market forces. They believed that government policies that combined price controls with programs that encouraged conservation and technological breakthroughs were self-defeating. On the one hand, artificially low prices encouraged energy use. On the other hand, conservation and R&D programs attempted to achieve energy savings and develop new energy supply technologies. With low energy prices the prospects of succeeding with conservation and R&D were not good, and contradictory policies made no sense.

In the immediate postembargo period the government maintained controls that lowered prices and equalized, or at least redistributed, the burden. There were three main reasons for government-controlled prices. First, there was the widespread belief that oil prices contributed to inflation. Second, the government favored achieving an equitable outcome over the efficiency that the market solution offered. Inflation and protecting the poor were not the only rationales for continuing with price controls that became increasingly complex as the decade progressed, however. A third reason was to protect people from the oil companies, which were seen as gaining enormous windfall profits from the price hikes. The government was supposed to prevent these companies from taking advantage of the crisis.

So strong was the opposition to higher energy prices that John Sawhill, head of the FEA under President Ford, was forced to resign because of his support for a 5-cent-per-gallon gasoline tax. The Energy Policy and Conservation Act of 1975 was scheduled to decontrol crude oil prices and end the entitlements program by 1981, but this provision was rescinded by Congress. Only toward the end of the Carter administration did a change in the attitude toward federal price controls take place. The administration attempted to raise the price of domestic oil to international levels, which again were in the process of tripling, owing to the Iranian crisis. The gradual phaseout of price controls along with a windfall profits tax were part of a political compromise—the windfall profits tax designed to capture some of unanticipated gains the oil companies were likely to realize from sudden price increases. The Reagan administration took steps to hasten full decontrol. The same 5-cent-per-gallon gasoline tax that forced John Sawhill's resignation was enacted into law with little controversy or notice in 1983.

Starting in 1978 with the deregulation of the airline industry, a broad deregulatory movement in the United States affected nearly every part of the economy. Energy deregulation was not restricted to oil. Partial deregulation of natural gas prices also took place. Because natural gas and oil competed in many markets, the market price for natural gas rose rapidly after the OPEC embargo. Before the embargo, there had been problems in sustaining an adequate supply; during the severe winter of 1972, for example, deliveries to existing customers had been curtailed and supplies rationed. From 1970 to 1978 nearly all net additions to supply went to the unregulated intrastate market, where prices were substantially higher than in the regulated interstate market. The FPC reacted slowly, allowing some increase in gas prices and trying to gradually achieve uniform national rates. Oil prices, however, were over $2.00 per Btu, having tripled since 1971, but in July 1976, the FPC only raised the ceiling price on post-1974 gas to $1.42 per Btu equivalent. Thus, newly available supplies continued to flow into the unregulated intrastate market with most supplies ending up in Texas (from whence they originated) where prices already were over $2.00.

New natural gas shortages were probably the most important reason for the growth in pressures for deregulation. These pressures counterbalanced consumer demands to maintain price ceilings and extend controls to all gas. In 1978 Congress passed the Natural Gas Policy Act (NGPA), which allowed natural gas prices to achieve greater parity with competing fuels. The act was also intended to enhance the development of new gas reserves. NGPA provided for the decontrol of new gas discovered after 1977 in 1985. In the meantime 17 categories of gas were created, with each given different price ceilings and escalation provisions. Most significant, the act extended price controls to the intrastate market, ending the two-tier system in which most of the new gas that was discovered flowed into the intrastate market. Even under NGPA, in 1985, 50% of natural gas still was subject to some type of price control; by 1990 this figure had been reduced to 25%. Pipeline companies absorbed the new gas prices by averaging them in with the lower costs of contractually priced supplies and passing through the difference to customers. Nonetheless, NGPA failed to anticipate the second oil price shock of 1979-1980, which led to increases in prices of fuels competing with oil that went far beyond the built-in escalation rates. The Reagan administration favored complete decontrol, but could not get a bill passed.

Along with deregulation of oil prices and partial decontrol of natural gas, some progress also was made in utility rate reform (Joskow, 1988). Electricity prices continued to be regulated at the state level, as utilities were recognized as natural monopolies for which price regulation was appropriate. But the Public Utilities Regulatory Policy Act (PURPA), passed in 1978, required that utilities sell power from one system to another at reasonable prices. Under the specific circumstances delineated in the act, they had to price power as a function of the costs it took to produce it and buy power from any supplier based on its marginal costs of production. In this way the government created a market for small power producers. In California, small power producers using unconventional means such as solar and geothermal took advantage of the situation, but in the rest of the country, most lacked the investment capital needed for projects.

Although growth in demand for power in most parts of the country did not warrant expansion of electric generating capabilities, still, the California development indicated increasing differentiation in the utility industry. A shift was taking place in the role of the utilities from producer of power to marketer and distributor. Pacific Gas and Electric indicated that almost all the new electricity the utility needed would be purchased from external sources, with alternative technologies playing a large role. Cogeneration, wind, and geothermal had made clear advances. California was the leader with nearly 1200 megawatts (MW) of alternative capacity installed in 1984 and 10,000 MW of capacity under construction or in an advanced stage of negotiation. These developments coincided with a decline in nuclear power. By 1985, close to 20% of all electricity generated in the United States came from nuclear power. Although total output had increased, production was far below forecasts and orders for new plants had fallen dramatically.

An Assessment of the Government Response

By the mid-1980s, imports had declined, but it was unclear what role U.S. government policies had played in bringing about the decline. With policies unfortunately working at cross-purposes, simultaneously stimulating and suppressing demand, the net effect was substantially diluted. The pluralistic political system responded to the demands of the claimants affected by the sudden energy price increases by trying to prevent the price increases from inflicting dramatic losses or costly, visible distributions (Tugwell, 1988). A complex system of compensatory intervention developed primarily to cushion consumers and producers from the impact of higher prices.

In the 1980s demand for energy leveled off. In 1973 it had been 74.2 quads and in 1979, 78.8 quads, but by 1983 it was down to 70 quads. Imports in 1983 were half the 6 million barrels per day imported in 1973. The United States, like other advanced industrial countries, had been learning how to conserve energy and was using less energy per unit of output. Some of the improvement was due to conservation policies, some to higher prices, and some to the economic recession that struck the United States and the rest of the world in 1979-1982. Oil from Alaskan fields started to flow, to some extent compensating for the continuing decline in production from the continental United States.

Consumers made life-style changes, learning to tolerate colder living and working conditions. They took actions like caulking and weather-stripping their homes and installing storm windows and doors. They also began to demand energy-efficient cars, buildings, and appliances. With slower economic growth came structural changes in the economy, a decline in large, heavy industry that used vast amounts of energy. There was change in the goods and services made and in the fuel mix. The electric power industry consumed 36% of total energy demanded, up from 27% in 1973, which meant a movement from oil and natural gas toward coal and nuclear energy. In addition to increased use of coal and nuclear power, there was more reliance on wood, geothermal, and other renewable energy sources.

Government energy policies contributed marginally to these trends. The 55 mph speed limit reduced traffic fatalities, but only saved about 200,000 barrels of petroleum per day (Tugwell, 1988). The fuel efficiency standard, which aimed to achieve a 27.5 mpg fleet average by 1985, saved about 405,000 barrels per day. Higher gasoline prices and concerns about gasoline availability also contributed to these results, however. Some 15 million households made energy conservation investments of some kind in 1978 and 6 million took advantage of government tax credits, adding up to annual savings of about 340,000 barrels per day; in this instance as well, higher prices and concerns about energy availability played as much of a role as government policies. A maximum of 1 million barrels of oil per day were saved by government policies. Some government policies had no effect whatsoever. The purpose of the Power Plant and Industrial Fuel Use Act of 1978 was to prohibit new electric power plants from using oil or natural gas, but coal already had a clear price advantage over oil and natural gas. The government conservation policies were often only symbolic, but the symbolism may have been important. In adopting various conservation policies, the government sent a message to consumers to get serious about energy savings. At the margin, without this message, some consumers might not have paid attention to the price changes and altered their behavior as rapidly or as thoroughly.

The real motivator of people was price and the real effect of government actions was felt via the price control and entitlement policies adopted initially as emergency measures in 1973 but which gained a momentum of their own and persisted until the early 1980s. Price controls caused the importation of an additional 900,000 barrels of oil per day and the entitlements program the importation of an additional 1.1 million barrels.

Altogether, the impact of price controls and entitlement transfers dwarfed that of conservation measures by a margin of at least two to one.

If U.S. policies in the immediate aftermath of the embargo were poorly conceived for their ostensible end, why were they undertaken? They were undertaken to shift the burden of the sudden rise in oil prices from consumers. The burden of the price increases fell greatest on the poor, those who lived in regions with the coldest winters and hottest summers, and those who dwelled in areas lacking local energy resources. The purpose of the price regulations was to protect these people. The entitlements program subsidized refiners to offset the sudden increase in the cost of imported oil. But price controls and entitlements yielded a substantial loss in economic efficiency. Oil companies were not willing to bring oil to the market. Thus there were shortages, with people losing time sitting in gas lines, making poor investment decisions because of the distorting effects of incorrect price signals, and purchasing the wrong type of equipment for their cars, homes, and factories. Administering the energy regulations was a costly and cumbersome effort. A small and temporary price cushion was created for consumers that partially protected them from the impact of the OPEC action with windfall profits taken from the holders of domestic reserves and transferred to companies with refining capacity.

On a political level an enduring impact of the policy changes was a realignment of interests. Few issues were subject to such intense and technically sophisticated scrutiny and few saw such fundamental conflict between values. Advocates of strong government action, certain of its effectiveness, called for decisive activity to alter consumption habits and reduce the nation's vulnerability to economic blackmail. Planners were opposed by adherents of a free market who considered the government itself to be responsible for the crisis and all the problems that occurred alongside it. The foundations of industrial society were called into question by the issues raised: equity, efficiency, growth, environmental protection, central planning, and decentralized control.

Producer and Consumer Interests: The White House and Congress

An important cleavage was between producers and consumers. Consumers stressed the illegitimate, hostile, and conspiratorial nature of the price increases. Producers considered it only appropriate that U.S. prices should rise to world levels. The executive branch of government tended to side with producers because it viewed price increases as part of the solution: Inasmuch as they had the potential to reduce consumption and lessen dependency on foreign sources, price increases contributed to national security. Consumers backed by a majority in the House of Representatives insisted that the price increases were the problem and that controls were the only means of protection.

The executive branch accepted a continuing affirmative responsibility for the energy system as a whole. It consolidated together data collection and analysis capabilities that had been scattered throughout the government and by means of a series of reorganizations created DOE. Congress too began to centralize decision making. In the House, the Commerce Committee became the central policy-making body for energy, but it still shared authority with several other committees and subcommittees. The Senate, under the leadership of Henry Jackson, a Democrat from the state of Washington, created the Committee on Energy and Natural Resources in 1977, which became the Senate's most influential policy-making body for energy.

Renewable Energy Movement

Outside the government numerous interest groups and lobbyists mobilized, representing diverse causes ranging from renewable energy and conservation to nuclear power and shale oil. One of the most influential advocates of the period was Amory Lovins, who became a catalyst for the renewable energy and conservation movement. His book, *Soft Energy Paths: Toward a Durable Peace* (1977), provoked an intense intellectual debate that challenged fundamental assumptions about U.S. society. Lovins's claim was that energy problems came about because of the excessive power of large corporations and government bureaucracies, organizations intent on using their massive power to impose expensive centralized technologies like nuclear power upon the unsuspecting public. The real solution lay in "soft path" technologies that were small scale, dispersed, and congenial. "Hard path" technologies like nuclear power led to a hard society that was authoritarian, militaristic, and inclined toward war. The soft path led to a society that was decentralized, diverse, peaceful, and self-reliant. Many of Lovins's predictions about the low cost of renewable energy were not realized, and his fundamental critique of U.S. society won few permanent sympathizers. Nonetheless, his views had a place among professional energy analysts and consultants who worked for the foundations and think tanks that produced major studies of the energy problem.

Business Interests

Business lobbying expanded as a result of the turmoil in energy prices. Depending upon the challenges encountered, business sectors followed different paths. Coal, being so abundant, appeared at first to have great potential, but these expectations proved illusory. A number of negative trends affected the coal industry. The alliance between union and management, which had controlled the industry and succeeded in increasing productivity by means of mechanization in the 1960s, disintegrated. In the 1970s, wildcat strikes were common and productivity declined. Productivity also was hurt by the passage of safety (the 1969 Coal Mine Health and Safety Act) and environmental legislation, which raised costs. Additional environmental legislation affecting coal was passed in 1977: the Surface Mining Control and Reclamation Act (SMCR) was signed into law by President Carter after it had been vetoed by President Ford. Productivity in the mines dropped from 19 to 14 tons per worker per day, a decline that lowered the relative cost advantage that coal enjoyed over other fuels. The 1974 Energy Supply and Coordination Act and 1978 Fuel Use Act both required that utilities switch from other fuels to coal, but they had little effect because growth rates in electric power demand were down and cancellations of new power plant orders common. Western coal, which had a number of advantages from low sulfur content to the circumstance of being surface-mined, did grow in importance. Strip mining was attractive even after the passage of SMCR, increasing from 15% of total production in 1973 to 36% in 1983. Utilities used 85% of the coal mined in the United States, up from 69% in 1973.

The integrated oil companies, which had lost direct control of their reserves to the producer governments, became buyers of offshore oil and increased their investments in other energy sources, nonenergy minerals, and unrelated economic activities. By the early 1980s, they owned about 40% of nongovernment coal reserves and from one third to one half of proven uranium reserves. Nearly 75% of domestic copper was in the hands of oil companies after the acquisition of Anaconda by ARCO. Mergers and acquisitions were common in the industry. Mobil bought Montgomery Ward, and Exxon purchased Reliance Electric. Texaco acquired Getty, Mobil bought Superior Oil, and SOCAL took over Gulf Oil. The ties the oil companies forged extended to other energy sources, different natural resources, and different lines of business. These ties meant that the objectives of the industry as whole became more diverse and complex. Once a monolith with homogenous interests, the industry took on a new look with new cleavages between firms reflecting their diverse holdings and ambitions. Independent retailers opposed the integrated companies that favored their own outlets. Small independent producers were exempted from the windfall profits tax and small refiners were favored by the entitlements program. Critics wanted the government to dismantle or radically restructure the industry. The industry's legitimacy was also hurt by scandals and major accidents. DOE, for instance, accused Exxon of improperly interpreting oil price regulations, and the company was ordered to pay damages of $2 billion.

Electric utility managers had been used to operating in a stable environment in which they could routinely pass on price increases to consumers. Now they faced hostile regulatory commissions suspicious of their requests for increases in prices (Joskow, 1988). They could no longer depend on steady, predictable increases in demand, nor could they rely on producing less expensive energy because of lower fuel costs, technological improvements, or scale economies. With higher prices, consumers started to cut back on demand. In 1974, average usage per customer declined for the first time in nearly 30 years. The utilities continued to invest in large plants, even though these no longer yielded economies of scale and were based on unrealistic assumptions about demand. High inflation rates, interest rate increases, and unexpected delays yielded huge cost overruns. The TMI accident altered public attitudes toward nuclear power and demonstrated that the uninsured costs of even a relatively minor accident could be catastrophic. Plans to construct new nuclear power plants were abandoned. Some utilities appeared to be on the road to insolvency. Earnings on equity deteriorated, stock values declined, bond ratings dropped, and indebtedness increased. (See Chapter 8 for a discussion of the future of the electric utilities.)

The Legacy of the Policy Changes

President Ford in his 1975 state of the union message predicted that by 1985 imports would account for over half U.S. oil use, but his prediction did not come true. Instead, in 1985, prices had eased, and the energy issue had receded from national prominence. Conventional wisdom was that the threat from the OPEC cartel was at an end and world energy prices would remain steady or continue to fall. OPEC was having trouble holding together in the face of declining demand and excess capacity (see Chapter 4). The experience since 1973 had shown that government programs often were misguided and frequently failed to accomplish what was intended, but that with deregulation market forces were having an important influence. When prices were high, people tended to use less energy, search for alternative supplies, look for more abundant sources to replace oil, and substitute other inputs for energy in production processes. Technologies were developed for more efficient energy use and purchases shifted to less energy-intensive goods and services.

Nonetheless, important questions remained about whether:

- The impact of lower prices would mean an end to the behavioral and investment changes that had occurred and a regression toward an earlier pattern
- Energy use per unit of GNP would continue to decline without more extensive behavioral changes or investments in expensive energy efficiency capital stock
- Technological developments that lay on the horizon would fundamentally alter the energy economy
- The creation of a strategic petroleum reserve would ease the pain of dealing with another embargo should it occur
- The rapid decline in U.S. oil production capability would lead to additional supply disruptions by the end of century
- Price stability would be possible given Middle East and Persian Gulf instabilities

PART II

4

The Organization of Petroleum Exporting Countries

The Organization of Petroleum Exporting Countries (OPEC) is a cartel that was formed in 1960 by Iran, Iraq, Kuwait, Saudi Arabia, and Venezuela. OPEC now includes 13 countries—Algeria, Ecuador, Gabon, Indonesia, Libya, Nigeria, Qatar, and the United Arab Emirates in addition to the 5 founding members. Of these 13 nations, 6 are Arab—Iraq, Kuwait, Saudi Arabia, the United Arab Emirates, Libya, and Algeria. Although Iran is not an Arab nation, it is Islamic and borders Arab nations. In 1967-1968, the Arab members of OPEC formed an exclusively Arab organization, the Organization of Arab Petroleum Exporting Countries (OAPEC). Syria and Egypt subsequently joined OAPEC. On October 17, 1973, 11 days after the armies of Syria and Egypt launched a surprise attack on Israel, OAPEC announced a cutoff of oil to Western countries and Japan. The 1973 oil embargo was one of the most dramatic actions taken by a cartel in history, catching nearly all observers by surprise and altering the course of post-World War II history. The pre-embargo era was marked by stable oil prices, assured supplies, and a flourishing world economy, whereas the post-embargo era has had unstable prices, uncertain supplies, and a floundering world economy. Other factors affected world economic conditions, and oil price rises only partially determined the results, but they did play a role (see Chapter 2).

On January 1, 1979, oil production in another OPEC nation, Iran, was almost entirely shut down because of the strikes and political disturbances that led to the overthrow of the Shah and the establishment of a fundamentalist Islamic republic. Iraq then invaded Iran, and on September 25, 1980, both countries started to bomb each other's oil facilities. The Iraqis damaged the Iranian refinery at Abadan—the world's largest—and the Iranians retaliated against Iraqi refineries at Basra. Oil tankers and freighters, trapped in the Shatt al-Arab waterway, had nowhere to go. Oil tanker traffic through the Strait of Hormuz was delayed because shipowners feared they would be caught in the conflict. With supplies reduced, the world again faced a major petroleum price hike.

Two principal perspectives have been advanced to explain cartel behavior (Teece, 1983). The first, an economic view, assumes that the primary motivation of cartels is to maximize members' wealth. Cartel members try to maximize the net present value of their revenues from an exhaustible resource until reserves from that resource are depleted (Aperjis, 1984). The other perspective on cartel behavior is a political one that assumes that cartel nations act to enhance their political power regardless of the economic consequences. Some (see Ahrari, 1986) argue, "OPEC's pricing behavior is essentially economic in nature" (p. 1), and see the overriding factor as the desire to maximize economic payoffs and minimize the undesirable effects from inflation, devaluations, and recession. But the political factor cannot be ignored. No matter what the effects of the 1973 Arab boycott were, the impetus for the boycott was political. The Iranian Revolution and Iran-Iraq War were not pursued for economic reasons. Indeed, by contributing to a worldwide recession, they weakened the hold of oil on the world economy. The collapse in world oil prices then devastated the economies of the OPEC countries (Brown, 1981; Gately, 1986a; Gately, 1986b; Ibrahim, 1982). So too Iraq's seizure of Kuwait cannot be understood from a purely economic point of view. The economic theory of cartel behavior misses the deep-seated political passions that affect the behavior of Persian Gulf nations. Thus, along with economics, it is necessary to consider political explanations for what OPEC does (Samii, 1985).

The Goals of the OPEC Nations

Conditions vary considerably among the OPEC countries. Some are democracies; some are dictatorships. Some are ruled by military juntas and some are governed by traditional monarchies. When the Cold War was at its height, some supported the Soviet Union and others were pro-American. In 1979, after OPEC was unable to reach an agreement on oil pricing, the Venezuelan oil minister Calderon Berti declared, "We are 13 countries, with 13 heads, 13 worlds, and 13 realities" (quoted in Aperjis, 1984, p. 182). Population, per capita income, and oil wealth divide the OPEC nations. There are over 150 million Indonesians and almost 100 million Nigerians, but only about 1 million people living in the United Arab Emirates, and only 200,000 in Qatar. Indonesia is a very poor country with GDP per capita under $500, whereas the United Arab Emirates and Qatar are very rich countries with GDP per capita above $20,000. Saudi Arabia, Kuwait, Iraq, and Iran have the largest crude oil reserves in the world. Indonesia possesses less than 6% of the proven Saudi reserves, and Nigeria less than 10%. Some OPEC countries have sufficient production capacity to generate oil revenues to meet their economic development needs, but others cannot meet their economic development requirements with oil revenues alone. Saudi Arabia, Qatar, the United Arab Emirates, and Kuwait belong in the former category; their oil revenues provide all they need for economic development. Indonesia, Nigeria, Algeria, and Venezuela belong in the latter category, with oil revenues insufficient to provide for their economic development needs.

OPEC nations that are able to finance their economic growth with their oil revenues have different economic interests than OPEC nations that cannot. As Sheik Ahmad Zaki Yamani, the former Saudi Arabian oil minister, described it, "Saudi Arabia's interests lie in extending the life span of oil to the longest period possible" to enable it "to build a diversified economy supported by industry, agriculture, and other endeavors" (quoted in Aperjis, 1984, p. 186). Nations like Saudi Arabia, which are rich in crude oil reserves, do not want prices rising to the point where alternatives to OPEC oil become feasible (Mead, 1986). They are likely to remain oil exporters for a very long time and therefore have an interest in preserving a healthy oil market over the long term. OPEC nations unable to finance their economic growth with their oil revenues have a different outlook: Their need is to generate revenues as quickly as possible. Their oil reserves are limited and their potential for future oil discoveries slim, so they do not care if prices rise to the point where it becomes feasible to develop alternatives. Sheik Yamani described their view as follows: "If I were an Algerian, I would certainly wish the price per barrel of oil to reach $100 this very day . . . and if by doing so I encourage and drive the world to invest in finding alternate sources of energy, such investments will not bear fruit in less than ten years, at which time the matter would be of no concern to me" (quoted in Aperjis, 1984, p. 186).

Because the nations with small reserves are not likely to be major producers in the future, they have no reason to consider Saudi Arabia's long-term interests. But the price increases they favor can be achieved only if such countries as Saudi Arabia keep oil from the market. The countries with small reserves are not in a position to achieve price increases on their own to help them maximize short-term earnings; thus, it has to be the nations rich in crude oil reserves that withhold the oil. For these nations to withhold oil depends on whether they can earn more money from doing so than from investing abroad. From 1973 to 1979, when oil prices went up more rapidly than the rate of return from investments abroad (Aperjis, 1984), it was in their interest not to produce oil. The rate of return on their investments did not match the rate of return from keeping oil in the ground. This situation reversed itself in the 1980s, however. When oil prices declined and interest rates on investments abroad increased, it was no longer profitable for these countries to withhold oil from the market. From a purely economic point of view, OPEC's cohesion diminished in the later period.

For economic reasons, Saudi Arabia, the United Arab Emirates, Kuwait, and Qatar can be expected to pursue a policy of moderation. These countries have extensive investments in the West and do not want to see Western economies hurt or the power of Western governments undermined. The political reasons for a policy of moderation are to maintain the support of the United States and other Western governments. These nations also rely on the United States and the West for military protection. Without weapons and other assistance, the survival of these regimes is in jeopardy. The threat comes from Arab extremists. Politically, however, association with the West is a liability because extremists in the Arab and Islamic world attack them because of it.

For some OPEC countries, economic calculations are not paramount. Iraq, Iran, and Libya are ruled by cliques hostile to Western pragmatism and materialism. (They would say western exploitation and power.) For them, economic prosperity is incidental to political ambitions. Oil can finance terrorism and be exchanged for weapons to fight the West. The ruling cliques of the oil-rich nations also are sympathetic to many of the causes of the extremists (e.g., Palestinian nationalism), supporting them monetarily and in other ways. Without hesitation in 1973, they used oil as a political weapon in a campaign against Western interests, and they remain vulnerable to political blackmail from the extremists. The premise of economic theory is that cartel members are rational, calculating economic actors that seek to maximize their material gain, but the reality of OPEC is that oil is used not only for the purposes of economic development but also for redressing political grievances.

Cartel Theory

In theory, a cartel is a group of sellers operating together to keep prices above competitive levels. The main way that the cartel accomplishes this end is to prevent goods from entering the market. If it withholds goods from the market, prices go up. Demand for petroleum does not change in the short run (it is highly inelastic), but adjustments are made in the long run (demand becomes more elastic). With the passage of time, people learn to use less petroleum. They conserve. They substitute other goods for the one whose price has risen. They shift their purchases from the product that the cartel has kept from entering the market to alternatives that by comparison become attractive as the first product's price rises. Maintaining collusion and policing the cartel under these circumstances are difficult. Ultimately, demand declines for the good that the cartel has withheld from the market, and with less demand for this good, prices fall. According to economic theory, most cartels fail in the long run even if they can have considerable impact in the short run.

Numerous cartels have existed for commodities traded on international markets. Copper, tin, bauxite, diamonds, chrome, phosphate, coffee, and bananas have all been subject to cartels, but most of them ultimately failed.

Cartels can fail for a number of reasons: They are inherently unstable. To increase the profits of cartel members, it is necessary to limit production. To do so, cartel members have to resort to collusion. They require an enforceable arrangement that curtails production. If they are unable to curtail production, cartel members cannot maintain high prices. But high prices undermine the cartel's ability to maintain its collusive arrangements, as they provide a strong incentive for nonmembers to expand production (Lowinger, Wihlborg, & Willman, 1986). Even if the cartel urges nonmembers to join, they are not likely to do so, as by staying out they can produce without controls and still benefit from the high prices the cartel has established. In effect, nonmembers are free riders who gain from the cartel's policies without having to pay the costs. Indeed, many of the world's large oil-producing states have not joined OPEC. Besides the United States, Canada, and the Soviet Union, non-OPEC producers include Mexico, Great Britain, Norway, Egypt, and Malaysia. From 1979 to 1983, the production levels of non-OPEC members reached record heights (Aperjis, 1984) even as OPEC, to support its official price structure, had to produce at 50% below capacity.

Another way in which high prices undermine the cartel is by dampening demand. When confronted by high prices, people tend to conserve. They buy less of the commodity the cartel is trying to control. High prices also undermine the cartel by encouraging people to find substitutes and inducing competitors to develop products that can be used instead of the product the cartel tries to control. In theory at least, cartels contain within them the seeds of their own destruction. In response to high prices, people search for alternative suppliers, reduce their use of the product, and try to locate substitutes.

When the market for a cartel's product diminishes, the problems of maintaining collusion grow. Under ordinary circumstances, collusion is not easy to maintain. Once a price is established, the cartel must decide how to distribute the total sales and profits, and any strategy chosen is likely to yield divergent benefits for different cartel members. One possibility is to simply fix the price and allow each member to sell at that price, but this option magnifies the advantages of low-cost producers. Another possibility is to establish quotas. High-cost producers, however, also do not like quotas, because these establish a limit on revenues. Relying on the relative sales of members in the precartel period or on the productive capacities of cartel members does not diminish the difficulties, as the choice of a base period and the measure of capacity become matters of dispute. Quota determination ultimately depends on bargaining and negotiation, which can breed mistrust and suspicion among cartel members. Differing political views exacerbate tensions derived from differing economic interests. In fact, devising a production allocation scheme acceptable to all OPEC countries has been anything but easy (Aperjis, 1984). Nigeria and Indonesia seek quotas allocated according to economic development needs and population, but the other OPEC members have maintained that shares should be allocated according to productive capacity and past market share.

Enforcing a production quota scheme, once accepted, is not easy, as the incentive to cheat is great. Production quotas have to be renegotiated periodically, and the renegotiation process also is difficult. When the market for a cartel's product declines, mistrust and suspicion increase. With less output and smaller profits, conflict grows among cartel members over the output and profits that remain. Under these circumstances, the temptation is great for individual cartel members to produce beyond their quotas and sell additional amounts of the commodity at discount rates without revealing to other cartel members what they have done. When cheating is rampant, cartel members have no reason for further cooperation. If everyone in the cartel sells at a discount, the cartel rapidly disintegrates.

Policing cartel members is difficult because subversion by individual members is very profitable. The availability of profits from cheating and the ease of making secret price concessions make it difficult to enforce cartel policies. A cartel member faced with a shrinking market, so far as price exceeds the cartel member's average minimum cost, will be inclined to embark upon competitive price cutting to increase its market share. Even in an expanding market, cartel members have an incentive to cheat: In an expanding market prices are rising, and high prices provide an incentive to explore, and exploration leads to the discovery of new supply. Cartel members cannot be expected to withhold from the market supplies that have been discovered at great cost. According to cartel theory, cartels cannot last long. If motivated purely by economic considerations, they eventually collapse as a consequence of their own internal contradictions.

Successes and Failures

These economic pressures have not been missing from OPEC history, and yet despite great duress, OPEC survives. The history of OPEC has not been that different from the history of other cartels; it has failed to function in an effective manner and has approached collapse. Yet OPEC has held together. The difference from other cartels is in how political events have impinged on OPEC's existence.

OPEC's Formation

Organized in 1960 following decisions by the major multinational oil companies to reduce oil prices, during the 1960s and early 1970s OPEC was quite weak. Its members complained of being exploited by the multinational oil companies. The multinationals feared the loss of their oil properties in the Mideast and elsewhere in the Third World. According to OPEC's reasoning, the multinationals were aware that their property rights in international oil were in jeopardy because of the decolonization process and nationalization; therefore, they were accelerating the rate of foreign oil production. The compound annual growth rate of oil production in the Mideast was 10.9% from 1960 to 1970, but much of this growth was attributable to rising demand to propel a rapidly growing world economy. From 1960 to 1970, oil prices rose only modestly. OPEC was frustrated that it could do nothing more than prevent the nominal price of oil from declining.

From 1970 to 1973 OPEC's position in world oil markets grew. Three quarters of the world's new oil discoveries in the post-World War II period were in Middle Eastern nations. OPEC production in 1973 was 31 million barrels per day, 80% of which it exported. It supplied over 80% of the free world's exports and controlled over 67% of the non-Communist world's oil supplies. World oil demand went up by about 8 million barrels per day from 1970 to 1973, but the non-OPEC supply increased by only 0.7 million barrels per day. The demand for OPEC oil expanded by nearly 7.5 million barrels per day. The five founding OPEC members (Saudi Arabia, Iran, Iraq, Venezuela, and Kuwait) raised their output to 6 million barrels per day, at which point they were operating near maximum sustainable capacity.

The price of producing oil in the Persian Gulf, where most of OPEC's oil was located, was only $1 to $2 a barrel. The Tehran-Tripoli agreement, which OPEC members reached in 1970, increased the market price of oil to $1.80 to $2.20 a barrel. An accelerating inflation rate offset the revenue increase to OPEC nations, causing a decline in the real price of oil. The breakdown in the Bretton Woods system and fall in the dollar's value compounded the real oil price decline. OPEC oil prices were denominated in U.S. dollars and a weak dollar decreased the purchasing power of the OPEC countries. Declining prices meant increased demand for oil without encouragement for the development of new supplies or for alternative forms of energy.

The 1973 Embargo

After 1973, oil prices evolved in a very complex manner in which politics played as much of a role as economics. Indeed, the evolution of oil prices can be divided into periods in which one or the other dominated. The period between 1973 and 1974 was one in which politics dominated. Between September and December 1973, OPEC's Arab exporting nations curtailed world oil production by 6.6%. The cutback in production came after the outbreak of the Arab-Israeli War in October of that year. OAPEC—the Organization of Arab Petroleum Exporting Countries, not the entire body of OPEC—instituted the embargo. Saudi Arabia initially cut production by 5% and stopped all shipments of oil to the United States. Saudi Arabia ultimately curtailed its production by 10% and then by 15%. Abu Dhabi, Libya, and Algeria also cut production by 10%, and Kuwait, Bahrain, Qatar, and Dubai did not permit oil shipments to the United States. In December 1973 Iran auctioned some of its oil at a price of $14 to $18 a barrel. Recognizing how high oil prices had risen, the gulf states promptly increased the price to $11.65 a barrel on January 1, 1974, creating average per barrel revenues of over $7. The real price of crude oil in 1973-1974 quadrupled.

On January 1, 1975, OPEC established the average government take for crude oil at $10.12 per barrel. According to economic theory, the consequences of setting oil prices at this level should have been rapid increases in non-OPEC oil production, massive conservation efforts, and substitution of other energy sources for crude oil. Specifically, what should have taken place was: extensive search for and development of new oil; lower demand for energy consumption; a more favorable environment for conservation; substitution of other cheaper fuels for oil; research into energy-saving technologies; and the development of alternative fuel technologies such as nuclear, oil shale, and coal and gas liquefaction. But the time lag between the price changes and the adjustments in supply and demand to new prices was considerable.

The United States was unprepared for the cutoff. It had no additional domestic oil supplies to which it could turn. U.S. production, after increasing at a compound annual growth rate in crude oil production of 3.2% between 1960 and 1970, declined at a compound annual rate of 2.75% between 1970 and 1976. Non-OPEC nations increased their net output. Oil output rose by 24%, showing that supply was not entirely price inelastic; prices were high but demand did not rapidly decline, showing that demand was relatively price inelastic. Consumption went down by a mere 10%.

From 1973 to 1977 OPEC had some success because short-run supply and demand were not completely responsive to the price changes. Nonetheless, as cartel theory would predict, the Arab oil producers who had initiated the embargo were not the main beneficiaries of the actions they had taken. Total OPEC production rose from 30.7 million barrels per day to 31.2 million barrels per day between 1974 and 1977, but non-Arab OPEC members expanded their output by 14.4% even as the Arab and Gulf states reduced their output by 13.5%. Mideast production actually declined from 21.9 to 20.5 million barrels per day. Nominal prices increased 16% from 1974 to 1977, but real prices, because the inflation rate was so high, went down 11%.

By 1977, the economic factors that cartel theory predicted would have an effect were working. There were substantial production increases from Mexico, the North Sea, and many small producers. The 16% decline in U.S. output from 1970-1976 came to an end when Alaskan production began. An increase of over 4 million barrels per day in non-OPEC production alleviated the pressure on oil prices. Demand for oil had been growing very rapidly before the 1973-1974 price increase, but afterward it tapered off. The OECD countries, which experienced the largest growth in demand prior to 1973-1974, had the greatest declines in 1974-1977. In the rest of the world, demand for petroleum grew at a slower pace, increasing by only 5 million barrels per day from 1973 to 1977, with nearly half the growth occurring in the United States.

The economic factors that bring about the decline of a cartel were starting to have an effect. Alternative sources of supply appeared. Demand leveled off. Real oil prices declined. Although nominal prices remained constant, inflation and depreciation of the dollar resulted in lower purchasing power for OPEC nations. The world had started to adjust to high oil prices in a manner consistent with economic theory. Markets were sticky in the short run, but they moved to increase supply and lower demand in the long run. Still, OPEC control of world energy markets remained strong. It continued to control 63% of the non-Communist world's oil supplies. Saudi Arabia, Kuwait and the smaller Gulf countries held over 60% of OPEC's productive capacity. As markets grew weaker as a result of higher 1973-1977 prices, OPEC's share of world crude production declined from 55.5% to 52.5%, but demand for its oil remained close to maximum sustainable capacity.

The Iranian Revolution and Iran-Iraq War

By 1977, the cartel had lost some ground, but no one anticipated what was to occur next—the Iranian Revolution and the Iran-Iraq War, which brought politics back to the forefront. The Iranians reduced production by over 2 million barrels per day from 5.5 million barrels per day to 3.5 million barrels per day. Their ostensible reason was to diversify their economy and make it less dependent on oil revenues. Iranian oil production actually did not exceed 3 million barrels per day during this period because of the technical, economic, and political impediments associated with the revolution. This shortfall drove prices upward, but total OPEC production remained about the same because other countries, especially Saudi Arabia, increased production to cover the difference.

Nonetheless, various countries, lead by Japan, tried to take precautions against a possible decline in the flow of oil from the Gulf. With Iraq's invasion of Iran, they feared the closure of the Strait of Hormuz and further price increases. Additional pressure on prices came from a buildup in oil stocks in purchasing countries of around 2 million barrels per day in 1979 and 1980. From 1978 to 1981, petroleum prices jumped from $14 a barrel to $37 a barrel, with the spot market exceeding official OPEC prices by $2 to $3 a barrel. By early 1981, the production of Iran and Iraq, which together had amounted to 8-9 million barrels per day, fell to 2.5 million barrels per day. Saudi Arabia and the United Arab Emirates were no longer able to take up the slack, and the net effect was a decline in oil production of nearly 4 million barrels per day.

Again, the economic system adjusted to the shock. World oil demand, which had reached a peak of 52 million barrels per day in 1979, fell. In the major industrialized nations it had already been slipping—from 35.2 to 31.1 million barrels per day between 1973 and 1980—as a result of energy savings and fuel substitution. The use of non-OPEC supplies, including natural gas from the Soviet Union, continued to grow. Decline in demand for OPEC oil between 1980 to 1982 was quite extensive, falling from 30 to 20 million barrels per day partly because of increases in non-OPEC supplies, but also because of falling economic growth rates, the deep worldwide recession of 1980-1982, and lagging responses to the 1973-1974 and 1979-1980 oil price increases.

The economic factors that lead cartels to their demise reasserted themselves. Economic theory predicts that in the face of declining demand cartels will have a difficult time maintaining themselves. As predicted, the new conditions prevailing in energy markets polarized OPEC. As demand declined and the Iran-Iraq War intensified, mistrust between the OPEC nations grew. They were unable to meet in November 1980 in Baghdad because of the war. Some called for a cease-fire, but neither Iraq, which was winning the war, nor Iran, which was losing, heeded the call to end hostilities. OPEC's radical camp consisted of

Iran, Algeria, and Libya. These countries vehemently opposed the United States and favored short-run OPEC revenue maximization to achieve political goals. The Gulf Cooperation Council, led by Saudi Arabia, made up the moderate faction. It sought a less restrictive pricing policy leading to long-run revenue maximization and wanted to protect OPEC's long-run interests. The remaining six OPEC members—Iraq, Indonesia, Nigeria, Venezuela, Ecuador, and Gabon—made up an independent group that was often divided.

Shrinking Demand: OPEC's Response

Shrinking demand for OPEC oil put pressure on the organization to reduce output. It established a ceiling of 17.5 million barrels per day in March 1983, then 16 million barrels per day in November 1984. The first price reduction in the 23-year history of OPEC occurred at the March 1983 London meeting, when prices were slashed from $34 to $29 a barrel. OPEC's plan to deal with declining demand was to designate Saudi Arabia to be the price setting residual supplier. Saudi Arabia could afford take on this role because it had expanded its market share from 24.2% to 30.4% of OPEC's production between 1973 and 1977. In 1982 OPEC decided that although other countries would be assigned a quota, the Saudis had to keep their production low enough to maintain the cartel's official price.

As the cartel's swing country, the Saudis were supposed to reduce output to maintain established price levels. This role was very disadvantageous to the Saudis. They saw demand for their oil fall by nearly 40% between 1979 and 1982. Between 1979 and 1985 all the OPEC countries had to cut output by at least 20%, but the Saudis experienced the greatest percentage reductions. Saudi production declined by more than 60% from 1979 levels. Kuwait's production also fell by nearly 60% and Libya's production dropped by nearly 50%.

Cartel theory would predict that when the cartel members cut back production, nonmembers gain; unrestrained from producing to maximize their revenues, they benefit from the cartel prices. Indeed, this is what happened, as from 1979 to 1985 non-OPEC oil supplies increased by more than 6.5 million barrels per day. The non-OPEC supplies came from Great Britain, Norway, Mexico, and the Soviet Union. Cartel theory also would predict that in a declining market cheating by cartel members is rampant. Shrinking demand generated pressure on individual OPEC countries to resort to so-called unconventional oil sales. By means of spot, netback, barter, and processing deals, the individual countries acted in their own interests to maintain and increase individual market share. The cartel was unraveling as a result of the bickering over production quotas and pricing policies and the efforts of individual members to maintain or increase market share in a shrinking market. Only Saudi Arabia and Algeria did not exceed the OPEC quotas established in December 1983.

At its January 1985 meeting in Geneva, OPEC established a new system to audit production, but this was never fully implemented and was disregarded by most member countries. As cartel theory predicts, in a declining market it is exceedingly difficult to police members and maintain collusion, and OPEC lost control of the market in 1985-1986. When dominated by economic factors, cartels are inherently unstable. The disunity within OPEC stemming from the Iran-Iraq conflict and other geopolitical considerations had broad implications as OPEC production slumped from a peak of 31 million barrels per day in 1979 to 16.5 million barrels per day in 1985. By the end of 1985 production reached a low of 15.5 million barrels per day. Below the agreed-upon ceiling, this level was no more than 40% of the non-Communist world's oil output. From 1981 to 1986, prices also went down, declining to $10 a barrel in August 1986. What happened shows how a cartel disintegrates when its members cannot stick to a market-sharing scheme. The power of the cartel wanes.

The expectation of the other OPEC members was that Saudi Arabia would continue to reduce production to prevent further price declines, but the Saudis became uncomfortable with the role of residual producer. Saudi Arabia's output continued to decline in the summer of 1985, to below 2 million barrels per day. Its revenue needs were not being satisfied, and it was exasperated that other OPEC members were cheating on their output quotas. The Saudis, like their neighbors in the Gulf, decided to increase their share of the oil market to maintain revenues. Saudi Arabia increased output above its quota level—6 million barrels per day—in 1986 demonstrating that it could keep prices down: It showed non-OPEC countries that unless they reduced oil output, the oil from their high-cost wells would be uneconomical to bring to the market. The Saudis were able to sell at low prices without suffering substantial revenue losses because the decline in price was offset by the increase in output. In taking the actions it did, Saudi Arabia risked hostile retaliation from the Iranians or Iraqis, who might widen the war in the Gulf, and from Libya, which threatened to use terrorism to destabilize Saudi Arabia internally.

OPEC Survives

With prices falling to $10 per barrel, the mood among OPEC members at their August 1986 meeting approached desperation. When adjusted for inflation, crude oil prices were below what they had been in the pre-embargo period. The decline in real oil prices meant dramatic decreases in OPEC revenue. And yet OPEC survived. Somehow it managed to forge a new agreement to limit production to the quotas established in December 1983. Cartel members honored their output quotas. Saudi threats were taken seriously. The price collapse of 1986 led to a strong recovery of demand, which arrested growth in non-OPEC supply. OPEC output increased by about 4 million barrels per day.

In December 1986, a new OPEC accord set prices at $18 per barrel. The return to a fixed pricing system depended on the reestablishment of working ties between Saudi Arabia and Iran. Many groups now had an interest in OPEC's survival. To be sure, non-OPEC producers showed no desire to break the cartel, because they also benefited from it, but banks, which had loaned billions of dollars to Mexico, Venezuela, and Nigeria, also counted on the cartel to prop up oil prices to secure their loans. The cartel had the support of many industrial nations who believed that it was necessary to maintain stable oil prices. A momentum built for OPEC's preservation that could not have been predicted by conventional cartel theory.

From 1986 to 1990, prices drifted upward. With less U.S. production, OPEC gained back market share it had lost. Despite the fact that world demand for oil declined, OPEC's influence grew. Then came the Iraqi-Kuwaiti dispute and OPEC again unraveled (see Chapter 1). Political circumstances, not economics, again determined OPEC's fate. Iraq, desperate for cash to rebuild its war-torn economy, resuscitated a dormant ambition to dominate OPEC and control world energy markets. OPEC countries were unable to resolve the dispute between Iraq and Kuwait, and Iraq invaded, taking over Kuwaiti oil fields and extending its control to 20% of the world's proven oil supplies. The world boycotted oil from Iraq and Kuwait, and petroleum prices shot up as high as $40 a barrel on spot markets. Prices rapidly fell, however, as the shortfall was made up by other OPEC members (Saudi Arabia, the United Arab Emirates, and Venezuela) and non-OPEC producers.

Backstop Technologies

Backstop technologies that can supply the energy markets supplied by oil provide an ultimate cap on oil prices (see Chapter 1). Saudi fears of high energy prices rest on the possibility that some of these backstop technologies might become commercially feasible. But commercial feasibility is a long way off: It could take a decade or more to expand capacity to successfully compete with oil. In the short run, backstop technologies provide no cap on oil prices, and OPEC prices can exceed the backstop costs.

Let us briefly review the potential of some of these technologies, starting with the most promising. Natural gas is the most promising alternative to petroleum for propelling automobiles, but storage and conversion problems remain to be overcome. Natural gas can be converted to methanol or gasoline, but the capital costs are high. Natural gas is so promising because it is cleaner burning that oil. With concern increasing about the greenhouse effect (see Appendix 2) and other environmental problems, natural gas has even more to offer than reduced dependence on uncertain foreign oil supplies. The nations of the former Soviet Union have vast natural gas reserves (they controlled over 40% of the world's reserves), and they will seek to release more natural gas for export to earn desperately needed foreign currency (Kanovsky, 1990). Western companies are anxious to work with these nations to help them develop their vast reserves. Also promising are the deposits in the Gulf of Mexico, but extraction problems would have to be overcome and production costs in this instance could be quite high. A major advantage of natural gas over petroleum is that it is more widely dispersed geographically and not as concentrated in countries with volatile political conditions. Even before the Gulf crisis, European consumption of natural gas was expected to rise more than 4% per year during the 1990s, about three times more rapidly than it did during the 1980s (Kanovsky, 1990). Much of the growth would be at the expense of oil consumption. The United States has approved a new gas pipeline from Canada that will displace about 100,000 barrels of oil per day.

Proven coal reserves in the United States are even larger than proven natural gas reserves. The heat content of the coal found in the United States is estimated to be nearly five times the heat content of recoverable crude oil reserves worldwide. Yet coal has severe limitations as a replacement for petroleum because it is not easy to create a product that can be used to propel automobiles. Synthetic gasoline can be made from coal at an estimated cost of about $1.60 a gallon. Coal gasification is also possible, at an estimated price of $11.92 per thousand cubic feet, which is about six times the market value of high-Btu natural gas.

The main use for coal is in electric power generation. For electric power to meet people's transportation needs, a new type of car—with cost and convenience features similar to gasoline-propelled vehicles—would have to be developed. An alternative would be to build electric-powered public transportation on a mass basis. Crude oil and natural gas no longer are commonly used for electric power generation, an outcome that has come about partially because of legal dictate and partially because of price considerations; it is simply not economical to use oil or natural gas to generate electricity. Besides coal, nuclear power and various unconventional technologies can be used to generate electricity. Depending on geographic location, the type of coal available, and environmental costs, coal has an advantage over nuclear in some places and nuclear has an advantage over coal in others. Comparing the social costs of coal and nuclear is very complicated. Coal involves real, here-and-now damage, whereas nuclear has a slight but very real possibility of catastrophic accident. Long-term nuclear waste storage problems have not been resolved; but coal is a major contributor to the acid rain and greenhouse gas problems. Hope may lie in the development of a new, "inherently safe" design for a nuclear reactor that would be much more forgiving than current models. Intermittent power can be provided by wind and solar power, but both require additional capital outlays for storage and backup peak power and neither has proven to be economically feasible on a large scale.

Nuclear fusion theoretically promises an inexhaustible potential source of power, but efforts so far consume more power than is produced. The tar sands in Alberta, Canada, offer an immediate, economically recoverable substitute for oil. If 10% ultimately is recovered, production will amount to 80 billion barrels of oil. Heavy oil in Venezuela could also become economically recoverable. Ten percent recovery would amount to another 100 billion barrels of oil. Oil shale worldwide, at 10% recovery, would yield nearly 2 trillion barrels of oil. At present, oil shale production costs are estimated to be about $60 per barrel of oil, and many environmental problems would have to be overcome to create a viable tar sands or oil shale industry. Alcohol can be used in a blend with gasoline or as a 100% substitute. It has been in use in Brazil since the 1930s, with costs per barrel estimated from $50.30 to $90.00 and per gallon from $1.20 to $2.14.

The Prospects for Oil

Future oil prices largely depend on the politics of the oil-producing countries. Realistically, wars, revolutions, and other upheavals interrupting supply have to be considered a real possibility because of the volatile characteristics of the regimes in the regions in the world where oil is found. If OPEC survives, the future will be different than if it does not. If it does survive, its actions depend on which group of countries are in a position to determine its policies. If the moderates, who care about the long-term viability of the world economy, prevail, outcomes will be different from a future dominated by the politically motivated extremists.

The balance of power within OPEC is just one factor in the world's energy future. Even without political uncertainty, market forces provide for instability. Relatively low energy prices in the short term contribute to world economic growth, but also dampen conservation efforts, discourage exploration and discovery, and tend to put an end to research and development on alternative technologies.

As the demand for OPEC oil increases, OPEC faces the choice of continuing to raise output at the same price or restricting it at higher prices. Either scenario assumes that OPEC is still around. Its control over energy markets can be weakened by additional discoveries of new oil and natural gas, continued momentum for energy efficiency, and increases in the availability of energy from alternative sources. The U.S. government and governments in other countries can help bring about these outcomes through public policy measures. Energy taxes, adopted for security and budgetary reasons, are the best type of action the government can take (see earlier chapters). If the government can assure an orderly increase in energy prices, then it can put pressure on producers to find oil and on consumers to use less of it.

5

Comparative Energy Policies

As Japan and France made substantial progress in decreasing their dependence on Mideast oil in the period following 1973, Great Britain became nearly completely independent of Mideast oil. Nonetheless, Japan and France probably adjusted better to the post-1973 situation. Great Britain benefited from major discoveries of oil in the North Sea, which made it virtually independent of foreign oil, although it had to divert substantial capital investment to develop the energy sector—capital that could have been used to bolster its declining economy. Moreover, Great Britain had trouble managing its energy industries, which were nationalized and had many inefficiencies. The Thatcher government's privatization program was only partially successful. Japan's adjustment consisted of many elements. It developed interests in countries and companies in the Mideast and elsewhere that had energy production capabilities. It charged up its export sector to help pay for higher energy bills. It stepped up conservation efforts and diversified the types of energy used, including the development of nuclear power. France adjusted to the post-1973 situation by stressing nuclear power and conservation. On a per capita basis, France became the world's leader in nuclear power production.

The lesson that can be learned from the experience of these countries is that energy self-sufficiency need not be the paramount goal of a country's energy policies. There are many ways a country can adjust to dependence on foreign sources of energy. Energy self-sufficiency is beneficial only if other conditions are in place to make an economy flourish. In this chapter, after reviewing the steps taken by Japan, France, and Great Britain, I examine post-1973 progress in the nations of the European Economic Community (EEC) as a whole. France and Great Britain are members of the EEC; Japan is not. The EEC, created in 1957 through the Treaty of Rome with six original members, now includes West Germany, Luxembourg, Belgium, Netherlands, Denmark, Italy, Ireland, Greece, Spain, and Portugal.

Japan

Japan is a great trading nation, but it produces only 0.2% of its total energy requirements. Next to the United States it is the largest consumer of energy in the world (Mossavar-Rahmani, 1988). Among industrialized nations, it is the most heavily dependent on foreign petroleum (Sakisaka, 1985). In 1983, it imported 65% of its oil from the Mideast. In that year, Japanese oil imports comprised 25% of the total exports from the Arabian/Persian Gulf nations. Japan's imports were more than twice the dollar amount of goods and services that it exported to the Gulf countries.

Japan coped with its energy dependence in a number of ways (Samuels, 1987). First, its national oil corporation, created in 1967 to lessen dependence on the international oil companies, set up overseas exploration and development ventures, making cooperative technical and economic agreements with most of the OPEC producers as well as many non-OPEC producers. By 1987 these joint exploration and production agreements with countries in the Mideast yielded about 10% of Japan's petroleum imports (Mossavar-Rahmani, 1988). Japan made numerous investments in the development of industry and infrastructure in the Gulf, and the Gulf states purchased large amounts of Japanese securities. Although Mideast imports did not fall below 65% (Mossavar-Rahmani, 1988), Saudi Arabia's share declined from about a third in the early 1980s to about a seventh in 1987. Japan had many reasons for desiring political stability in the Mideast (see Chapter 1 for a discussion of Japan's response to the 1990 crisis in the Gulf). Japan's energy investments in Southeast Asia, Mexico, and other areas where oil is found have not been as successful, and it has fewer interests in these regions.

Energy and raw materials prices (along with exchange rates, which have a large impact on these prices) are very important to the Japanese economy. Japan has paid for the high level of energy and raw materials it imports by expanding exports (Ramstetter, 1986). With the exception of the first 2 years after 1973, Japan succeeded in maintaining trade surpluses and controlling the inflationary pressures of energy price increases. In 1983 it exported nearly twice the dollar value of goods to the United States as it imported (Sakisaka, 1985). It was so successful at establishing a trade surplus with the United States that this surplus became a major source of friction in its relationship with the United States. U.S. energy exports to Japan in the form of coal and liquified natural gas (LNG) constituted about 8% of total U.S. exports to Japan. The United States also collected fees from Japan for uranium enrichment and the licensing of light water reactor technology. But U.S. energy exports to Japan could grow only if the United States made a major breakthrough in a technology that Japan needed.

After the oil embargo, energy became Japan's most important domestic political priority (Ramstetter, 1986). Japanese policies, which aimed to reduce demand and diversify energy sources, succeeded in decreasing Japan's dependence on uncertain foreign sources. Economic growth declined after the 1973 energy price hike, averaging slightly less than 4% per year in 1973-1983 after average annual increases of nearly 10% in 1963-1973; the connection between economic growth and energy consumption weakened, however (Sakisaka, 1985). Oil consumption fell by 20%, from 5.1 million barrels per day in 1973 to 4.2 million barrels per day in 1985 (Mossavar-Rahmani, 1988). Production in basic materials, particularly aluminum and petrochemicals, stagnated because world economic growth was weak and the competitiveness of Japanese industry, given higher energy prices, declined. Japanese economic growth took place in processing and assembly industries and in the expanding service sector, which were less energy intensive. Energy conservation became more common in transportation and in household and commercial heating. Improved production equipment was installed. Finally, recessionary conditions played a role in the movement away from petroleum (Ramstetter, 1986).

The Energy Rationalization Law of 1979 was the basis for Japan's energy conservation efforts. It provided financing for conservation projects and a system of tax incentives to promote conservation (see Chapter 1). Over 5% of total Japanese national investment in 1980 was estimated to have been for energy-saving equipment (Mossavar-Rahmani, 1988), and in the cement, steel, and chemical industries over 60% of total investment was for conservation. Between 1982 and 1983, the Japanese Ministry of International Trade and Industry (MITI) revised its forecast of Japanese petroleum consumption downward. By 1995 oil was expected to provide only about 50% of Japan's energy needs, down from 62% in 1982. Nuclear would provide 14% and LNG 12%, each up from 7% in 1982.

Thus, in addition to using less energy, Japanese society shifted from petroleum to other forms of energy, particularly nuclear power and LNG. Japan's nuclear program had close ties with the United States. The Japanese licensees Hitachi and Toshiba introduced the General Electric boiling water reactors; Mitsubishi introduced the Westinghouse pressurized water reactors. The U.S. Export-Import Bank funded Japanese nuclear power stations at generous credit terms. In contrast to the United States, Japan's nuclear industry tried to lower construction costs with standardization and other measures. After overcoming early operating problems, the load factor of Japanese nuclear power plants was among the highest in the world. As of 1988 Japan had 35 units with nearly 28,000 MW capacity. It was fourth behind the United States, France, and the Soviet Union in total nuclear capacity. Twelve units were under construction and four were in the planning stages. Japan was developing its own light water reactor and domestic fuel cycle operations to limit reliance on the United States. It had plans for an advanced 600 MW thermal reactor and for small reactors that used helium gas for district heating and industrial processes as well as electric generation.

LNG use also rapidly increased in Japan. Japan was the world's largest market for LNG in 1986, accounting for three quarters of global LNG shipments. Most Japanese LNG originated in Indonesia, with alternative suppliers in Thailand, the Soviet Union, and Canada. Japan also participated in LNG developments in Australia and the Mideast. LNG was attractive particularly for electricity production in close proximity to big cities because it burned efficiently and was nonpolluting. LNG required heavy capital investments, however, and to guarantee a supply necessitated long-term contracts of 20 years or more. The price of LNG declined in the mid-1980s, being linked to petroleum prices. Also because of the linkage to petroleum prices, the price was unstable, however. Moreover, LNG was more expensive for power production than either nuclear or coal.

Coal was expected to play a more important role in Japan in the latter part of the 1990s. Japan would have to decide how to allot orders to the

United States, China, Australia, Canada, South Africa, and other suppliers. Its domestic coal industry, declining for many years despite heavy subsidies, was plagued with problems and never developed substantial production capability. Coal's role in Japan would not be great unless nuclear power plant operating costs skyrocketed or coal costs greatly declined.

Lower oil prices had very important effects on the Japanese economy. Prices started to decline in constant dollars in 1982 and in yen in 1983. The decline continued through 1986, dropping below $13 a barrel. In 1981, fuel and natural resource imports constituted more than 50% of Japan's total import bill. Crude oil made up more than 35% of this total. By 1986, these figures had been cut in half, with petroleum amounting to just 15.7% of Japan's total import bill (Ramstetter, 1986). Lower oil prices created additional demand for oil (Mossavar-Rahmani, 1988). In particular, the demand for transportation fuels went up. Gasoline demand increased by 2.5% in 1986 from 1985 levels, because more cars were on the road, they were bigger, and they were being driven more miles. Demand for jet fuel also increased, as did demand for other petroleum products. Because of the appreciation of the yen, however, the Japanese were not spending substantially more for energy. But forecasts for energy use had not taken into account the increasing demand for energy (Mossavar-Rahmani, 1988), and when prices suddenly declined, orderly implementation of Japan's long-term energy plans was disrupted.

France

France's energy resources are extremely limited (Giraud, 1983). It possesses some natural gas, coal, and hydropower, but together these energy sources constitute a minute fraction of the world's total production. By 1973, oil made up 67% of the total energy used in France, up from 25% in 1960. French dependence on foreign energy had grown to 76.2%. Since World War I France had been aware of its dependence on foreign energy and had taken steps to overcome it. It owned stock in the Iraq Petroleum Company, which discovered oil in that country in 1927, and French national oil companies helped develop the oil resources of the former French colonies in North Africa.

Political instability in the Mideast and North Africa led France to take a leading role in the development of civilian nuclear power after World

War II. In 1945 de Gaulle set up the French Atomic Energy Commission (Commissariat a l'Energie Atomique, or CEA) to develop the military and peaceful uses of nuclear power. By the end of the 1960s, however, civilian nuclear power had made few advances in France. The gas graphite reactor upon which the French relied had not proven itself technically or economically feasible. The French utility, Electricite de France (EDF) insisted that CEA abandon this technology and adopt the pressurized water reactor (PWR), which had proved more successful in the United States. EDF had to obtain a license from Westinghouse to use the PWR. It obtained licenses to use other aspects of U.S. technology, including methods of uranium exploration, production, and enrichment; fuel reprocessing; and finally the fast breeder reactor. Still, the program was proceeding at the very slow pace of around one reactor per year at the time of the 1973 energy shock. The story of the French energy program after the 1973 energy embargo has two primary elements—the rapid growth in France's reliance on nuclear power and the largely successful efforts France has made in the area of conservation.

The French nuclear program took off after the embargo. The French government committed itself to the construction of six 900 megawatts electric (MWe) reactors per year, the rationale being that nuclear energy was the only form of power that could be developed with French resources—France had 120,000 tons of uranium reserves—at a reasonable cost. The French developed capabilities in all areas of the nuclear power cycle. Framatome, a private company of which CEA owns about a third, became the French Westinghouse, designing reactors with EDF and supplying the nuclear steam supply system. EDF acted as its own architect-engineer, supervising companies constructing the reactors. COGEMA, a CEA affiliate, managed the different parts of the fuel cycle. Its activities covered the entire array of nuclear fuel cycle processes from uranium enrichment to waste treatment. French commitment to nuclear power extended to commercialization of the fast breeder reactor (the Phenix and Superphenix facilities), a project that the United States abandoned in the mid-1970s.

By 1990 over 70% of France's electricity came from nuclear power. More than 50 reactors had been constructed. The average construction time was a little under 6 years, whereas in the United States the average construction time was nearly 12 years. France exported electricity to nearly all its neighbors, keeping its rates among the lowest in Europe. Domestic consumption of energy had increased at an annual rate of about 6% from 1980 to 1990 as economic growth grew annually at an average rate of 3.5% and consumption of electricity took off because of the relatively low energy prices. French success could be attributed to a variety of factors: standardization in design and construction; greater sensitivity to the consequences of oil dependence; centralization of activities in EDF, Framatome, the CEA, and their affiliates; technical confidence; the competence and sophistication to run a technology with high risk potential; and the political will to carry out the nuclear program.

After the period of intense construction ended, the aim shifted to running existing plants safely and efficiently. At the time of the 1973 energy crisis, no one foresaw an end to nuclear development. It was thought that a growing need for energy and the limited availability of fossil fuels would yield a continuing need for nuclear power. But in 1990, the French government finally called for a period of consolidation. Investment declined and new construction came to an end. *Les nucleocrats,* as the officials responsible for nuclear power in France were known, were concerned. The classic solutions to the transition problems that French nuclear power faced were laying off workers and reorganizations. The future unity of Europe constituted the principal chance for the sector's renewal with one of the main opportunities being a common all-European reactor.

No one can doubt that France made remarkable progress in exploiting nuclear energy. French progress extended to another area as well—conservation (Jestin-Fleury, 1988). From 1973 to 1980 the French economy grew by 22%, the number of cars increased by 20%, and the number of homes equipped for heating grew by 50%; yet energy and oil consumption only increased by 7%. Between 1975 and 1986 GDP went up by 27%, but energy demand grew by just 13%. Substantial conservation gains were made in manufacturing, and somewhat lesser progress in the residential and commercial sectors and transportation.

In manufacturing, producers responded to price signals by reorienting output toward less energy intensive activities. Starting in 1976 the government, through the Energy Conservation Agency (AEE), subsidized 3100 projects at a cost of more than Fr 8.4 billion. These subsidies were particularly effective in motivating companies that might not otherwise invest in energy conservation. The subsidies came to an end in 1980, however, when they were replaced by tax deductions meant to last until 1985. French companies expected 2-3 year payback periods on their energy conservation investments, but in 1987 after energy prices had fallen, the payback periods rose to 4-5 years and became a strong disincentive for further investment. Manufacturing conservation generally focused on new heat pumps, energy exchangers, processes to recover waste heat or waste by-products, technologies to control energy flows, new manufacturing processes, and better insulation. The manufacturing sector moved toward greater use of electricity, which saved energy when 1 kilowatt-hour (kwh) of electricity was substituted for more than 2.5 kwh of fossil fuels.

In the residential and commercial sectors, the government mandated lowering temperatures in public buildings from 20°C to 19°C for a saving of 7% of the annual heating oil supply. The conservation agency also made agreements with 8500 small businesses to market home energy conservation improvements. Factors that yielded conservation were higher prices, government incentives, regulations and standards for new buildings, and forecasts about long-term energy prices. These factors resulted in retrofitting of existing dwellings, construction of new homes with more insulation, and the replacement of boilers by more energy-efficient ones. Progress was offset by increases in the number of people and number of dwellings, the growing adoption of central heating, an increase in the number of homes with water heaters, and the growing use of electric appliances. More single family houses were constructed in France during this period, using more energy for heating because of more wall space exposed to the outside. The new houses also tended to use more energy because they were larger than older dwellings. New appliances tended to be more efficient, but their adoption was very widespread. More French people had refrigerators, freezers, clothes washers and driers, dishwashers, and televisions, all adding to energy consumption.

The goal in transportation was to increase average gasoline mileage from 26.7 mpg in 1979 to 39.2 mpg in 1990. Experimental vehicles achieved 60 mpg and 80 mpg, and a media campaign urged people to drive less and drive more efficiently. New speed limits were placed on all the major highways. The number of vehicles grew from about 15 million in 1975 to 21 million in 1986, but the average distance driven per year went down slightly from 13,200 km per vehicle per year in 1975 to 12,800 km per vehicle per year in 1986, and the number of vehicles using diesel fuels rose from 300,000 in 1975 to 2.1 million in 1987.

As a result of greater reliance on nuclear power and conservation, France by 1986 was 46.2% reliant on national sources of energy. This accomplishment was very close to the goal of 50% energy self-sufficiency by 1990. How much of this change, however, was permanent?

As oil prices declined, behavior could revert to old patterns, but technical progress would remain even if investments in new energy-saving technology became less common when the French government ended its extensive program of incentives and subsidies for energy conservation.

Great Britain

In the 16th century England faced one of the world's earliest energy crises. Deforestation ended its capability to provide its energy needs. It adjusted by becoming the world's largest producer of coal (Carter, 1986). By the 19th century, its coal production was six times the rest of the world's coal production combined. Along with such innovations as James Watt's steam engine, coal was the catalyst of the industrial revolution, which began in Great Britain. Great Britain was also the home of other innovations in energy use, from natural gas for lighting to Michael Faraday's invention of the modern dynamo, which made possible the generation of electric power.

During World War I, Great Britain was vulnerable to interruptions in petroleum supply. After the war, therefore, the British companies British Petroleum and Shell took the lead in the international search for new sources of oil supply; they played a major role in developing oil in the Mideast, in what were then British colonies.

After World War II, Great Britain lost most of its colonies and turned its search for oil and natural gas to the North Sea. With the discovery of natural gas in the North Sea in the 1960s, Great Britain became heavily dependent on natural gas. It built a national pipeline and signed a long-term contract with the government company for the provision of natural gas at relatively low prices. In the mid-1980s, the British consumed about a quarter of the natural gas used in Western Europe. Natural gas constituted about 40% of the total energy used in Great Britain, with electricity, coal, and oil sharing the rest of the market about equally.

After the 1973 energy price shock, oil was reserved for premium uses, and coal made something of a comeback after having been in decline for a considerable period. In the middle of the 1970s came major discoveries of oil reserves in the North Sea, and Britain regained its energy self-sufficiency. The consequences for the British economy have been mixed. Great Britain and Norway, the countries that made the

North Sea finds, enjoyed low annual growth rates for energy prices (Bending, Cattell, & Eden, 1987). From 1978 to 1984, the average price increases in Great Britain were 3.9% and in Norway 4.1%. These figures compare with price jumps in the United States of 4.8%; in West Germany, 5.5%; in France, 5.6%; in Japan, 6.6%; and in Italy, 6.8%. The tax revenues from energy in Great Britain amounted to £131 billion in 1985. Although total capital investment as a proportion of output fell in almost all the industrialized nations after 1973, investment due to energy rose, a trend that was most marked in Great Britain and Norway. Energy investment in Great Britain, however, constrained manufacturing investment, which the declining British economy desperately needed. Between 1974 and 1981, the largest declines in manufacturing as a proportion of GDP among industrialized nations were in Great Britain and Norway, the countries that had advanced the most toward energy self-sufficiency, because of their North Sea discoveries. Japan and Italy, in contrast, increased manufacturing's role in GDP, and in West Germany, France, and the United States the decline was not as severe as in Great Britain and Norway. In Great Britain, energy investment grew at the expense of manufacturing and construction. In Norway, it grew at the expense of services. Access to North Sea oil also led to the appreciation of the pound sterling against the dollar, dampening the exports of manufactures and increasing imports, which further hurt the already strapped British economy.

In comparison to other nations, Great Britain had old capital stock, low industrial investment, and low labor productivity, which drove down its international competitiveness even as the country achieved greater energy self-sufficiency. Great Britain could not escape the vicious cycle of low investment, low productivity, and low economic growth that contributed to continued low investment. During the world recession of the late 1970s and early 1980s, it retired much outdated capital stock, reducing output and increasing unemployment, and in this way productivity went up; but it had to give up on much of its basic manufacturing base because developments in the energy sector absorbed capital that might otherwise have gone into manufacturing. Although the development of new energy reserves in some ways contributed to Great Britain's economic growth, it also discouraged economic revitalization by competing with other industry for capital and because of effects on exchange rates that hurt the country's international competitiveness.

Moreover, Great Britain's energy industries were nationalized and very inefficiently managed, which meant diversion of capital and resources from potentially dynamic, growth-oriented sectors of the economy to a stagnant and backward sector. Because of the precarious supply situation during World War I, the British government took a majority interest in British Petroleum, nationalizing the industry in order to play a leading role in the search for new oil (Carter, 1986). After World War II, the Labor party came to power on a platform that promised to nationalize Great Britain's remaining coal, gas, and electricity industries. Partly for ideological reasons and partly for wartime reconstruction, it created the National Coal Board (NCB), British Gas Corporation (BCG), and Central Electricity Generating Board (CEGB). In the 1970s after the discovery of oil reserves in the North Sea, the British National Oil Company, a government corporation, was established. It produced about 7% of North Sea oil and ultimately handled about 60% of the oil produced there. Thus, all the energy sectors in Great Britain—oil, coal, gas, and electricity—had been either partially (oil) or completely (all the other sectors) nationalized.

In the period of rising energy prices, the nationalized energy industries faced trade-offs that were difficult for it to handle effectively because its decision-making calculus was influenced by public interest considerations. For example, financial costs had to be kept down at the same time that there were pressures to keep open uneconomical coal pits because of the social and national security costs of closure. Another difficult trade-off was balancing the immediate social benefits of maximum North Sea exploitation versus the long-term benefits of slower development. The British government tried to steer a middle course. Its central planners were unconstrained by market forces. Neither all-knowing nor all-seeing, they used a combination of pricing policies, taxes, and incentives to influence the nationalized industries. The nationalized industries had a statutory obligation to supply all customers and not to engage in cross-subsidization or predatory pricing. They were supposed to break even based on 2-year moving averages, and to adhere to 3- to 5-year financial targets. The government made an annual review of corporate plans and investments and allowed a reasonable rate of return of about 5%. The nationalized industries had to limit their indebtedness to the national government, control unit costs, and price the services they offered to cover accounting costs. The goal was to simulate the desirable effects of the market by relating prices to long-run marginal costs, but this goal was difficult to accomplish. In effect, the aim was to simulate the market without really being affected by market forces. In most energy-producing sectors, efforts to achieve the government goals had to be based on highly imperfect information and subjective estimates. Only in the electric power industry was something approaching long-run marginal-cost pricing achieved via time-of-day tariffs.

Government relations with the nationalized industries deteriorated. The government's interests differed from those of the industries, and it intervened to pursue macroeconomic objectives such as price restraint or to stimulate investment at times of unemployment. Decision making in the nationalized industries was highly politicized. The electric and gas industries had substantial operating profits, and they could finance their capital requirements from their revenues; but profits in the coal industry were poor, the work force was unionized, and opposition to the closure of uneconomic mines was great. It was estimated that 90% of mining losses came from 30 of the 190 pits in Great Britain, but closing these mines was very difficult. What the private sector could do with impunity, government-managed industries were constrained from carrying out. Only after 1984-1985 were some mines closed and productivity enhanced. In another area, new power plant construction was poorly managed. Costs for comparable coal-fired power stations were twice as high in Great Britain as in France or Italy. The government monopoly made excessive investments at poor rates of return. With respect to natural gas, the government was reluctant to raise prices to cover costs. Average-cost pricing of natural gas did not take into account that new gas was more expensive to produce than old gas. This type of pricing meant that depletion of domestic natural gas reserves occurred too rapidly.

The Conservative party proposed that the British nationalized energy industries be completely privatized, but encountered trouble in carrying out this plan. With the exception of coal, the energy industries had natural monopoly characteristics—economies of scale and the need to prevent duplicate investment in fixed infrastructure. Therefore, if privatization were to occur, there was a need to develop a strong regulatory apparatus to counter the capability of the energy industries to take advantage of consumers and earn excessive profits. But the British government under the Conservative party did not have the inclination to create new regulatory agencies. Moreover, it lacked the budgetary funds to create new bureaucracies where none existed. The Conservative party platform called for privatization and regulation to deal with the natural monopoly characteristics of these industries, and the government took some steps toward privatization, but in only one area carried its program to completion. The British National Oil Company was abolished and its assets were transferred to the private companies Britoil and Enterprise Oil. In other areas, deregulation similar to that occurring in the United States was tried. The gas company was compelled to run its pipeline system as a common carrier, which meant that anyone with natural gas to ship could have access. The electric company had to allow private companies to generate power and to use its transmission lines. But because of the high costs of market entry and because the incumbent companies had long histories of statutory protection from competition, they were able to withstand these challenges to their market power. The results in Great Britain were in sharp contrast to the results in, for example, California, where over 25% of electric supply was generated by private parties who had been outside the system prior to deregulation.

The Conservative Party proposed complete privatization of the gas company, but the regulatory powers of the government were too weak to protect the public. The Office of Gas Supply was supposed to oversee pricing, which would be based on interfuel competition. The Office of Fair Trading would play a role, and consumer complaints would be heard by the Gas User's Council. The looseness of regulation and its fragmentation made the plan questionable in the eyes of many British politicians. Before interfuel competition would be effective as a check on prices, import-export restrictions had to be liberalized. Privatization was based on the assumption that fuel switching was easy, but fuel switching was possible only in the industrial sector and even in this sector only a small number of firms had the capability to switch fuels. Even when they did switch, it required time to implement the change. Predatory pricing became a distinct possibility. The new gas company could make major North Sea acquisitions with its profits and reduce the number of companies in exploration and development. Thus, although Great Britain achieved energy self-sufficiency, it did not experience the boost to its economy that was expected. Too much investment was diverted to a very inefficient sector of the economy, and needed reforms in this sector of the economy were hard to accomplish.

Energy Efficiency in the EEC

Since 1973 all the EEC countries except Greece and Portugal have become more energy efficient (Jochem & Morovic, 1988). The British response to the 1973 crisis was less vigorous than that of other countries because of the North Sea oil discoveries and other impediments in the British economy. The West German response to the 1973 crisis was more vigorous than that of other EEC nations. But after 1979, energy intensity declined more rapidly in the other EEC nations than it did in West Germany (Bending et al., 1987). Electricity intensity grew in the EEC countries, but this growth slowed after 1979. In France, the growth in electricity use was greater than in other EEC countries, reflecting the French preference for nuclear power. Declines in energy consumption in 1979-1982 occurred partly because of higher energy prices and partly because of the economic stagnation that hit industrial production particularly hard (Jochem & Morovic, 1988). Short-term changes in energy consumption took place because of the climate and the business cycle. Long-term changes were structural or involved energy efficiency improvements.

The greatest improvements in energy intensity came from energy efficiency gains, 2.5% per year in 1979-1983, but only about 1.1% in 1984. Technical improvements from higher efficiency engines dropped off by 1984 as people demanded bigger cars, reduced vehicle occupancy, and ignored speed limits. In the residential sector, energy intensity increased because central heating became more common, together with single family dwellings and electrical appliances. By 1984 the prices of energy were stable and economic growth resumed. Industrial production increased and energy consumption grew. The period of stable and declining energy prices from 1984 to 1986 led to a reversal in the energy conservation process. Because of budgetary reasons most government energy conservation programs diminished. With declining energy prices, sustaining the energy efficiency gains of the previous period became highly uncertain.

Long-Term Prospects in the EEC

Increased oil consumption played an important role in the reconstruction of post-World War II Europe. In the 1950s, oil use in Western Europe increased by a factor of 20, whereas energy use generally grew by a third (Lonnroth, 1983). The conjunction of positive forces, however, came to an end in the 1970s. Predictions about the long-term prospects for energy in the EEC often have been wrong. After the second oil price shock, forecasters estimated that OPEC would be producing at a level of 30 million barrels per day indefinitely, but in the mid-1980s OPEC's production fell below 20 million barrels per day. In 1981, EEC nations imported more than 80% of the oil they used, mostly from OPEC countries. They consumed about a third of the world's total exported volume. Future supplies would depend on numerous factors, not the least of which would be: the price of petroleum, the policies of OPEC and non-OPEC oil-producing countries, the development of non-OPEC supplies, the claims of other regions in the world for oil, political stability in the Mideast and other energy-rich areas, and the potential development of high-cost alternatives to oil.

If OPEC production was 20 million barrels per day in the year 2000, the EEC countries could face a shortfall of about 20%. They could make it up from expanded coal production in Great Britain and the Federal Republic of Germany, but it is unlikely these countries would provide the difference as they already had closed down old mines that were uneconomical. Additional coal could come only from the United States, Australia, and South Africa, but to be cost-effective, imports from these countries depend on the development of new technologies and the expansion of ports, railways, storage facilities, and ships. Strict environmental regulation, particularly concern about acid rain and the buildup of carbon dioxide in the atmosphere, limits the potential for the expanded use of coal.

Natural gas is another possibility for making up the shortfall. Western European nations produced about 85% of their own gas in the early 1980s. The rest of their natural gas came from the Soviet Union (10%), Algeria (3%), and miscellaneous sources. The Netherlands, which was the biggest West European producer (48%), was scaling down its production because of rapid depletion. It was likely to be able to provide only 13.5% of West European needs by the year 2000. The British contribution could climb from 20% to a maximum of 26% and Norway's contribution could grow from 14% to a maximum of 34%, based on exploration and additions to North Sea reserves by these countries. Still, an additional 13% of demand would be needed. Imports from the former republics of the Soviet Union and Algeria would have to increase. The former Soviet republics had to raise their capacity to supply the EEC from 13.5% to 22%, and Algeria from 7% to 10%.

The further expansion of nuclear power production in Western Europe is unlikely and solar, wind, and biomass have limited potential without a technological breakthrough. Western Europe, therefore, faces the prospect of limited energy growth until the year 2000. Adjusting to such a low level of energy growth could be difficult. At current levels of energy consumption, the present standard of living in EEC nations can be sustained with lower levels of energy input only if more efficient production methods are used.

PART III

6

Synfuels

Interest in synthetic fuels is very old. During World War II, the Germans made advances in synfuels development. From 1945 to 1958, as the United States shifted from primary dependence on coal to dependence on natural gas and oil, plans for a coal-based synthetic fuel industry disintegrated because of the cheap flow of foreign oil (Vietor, 1984). This shift occurred despite the poor economic condition of the coal industry and the country's growing dependence on foreign oil. From 1959 to 1968, the government was able to maintain only a "feeble" pilot plant program for coal-derived synthetic fuels (Vietor, 1984). As long as there was ample foreign oil, synfuels were not economically attractive.

In 1973, however, in response to the Arab boycott, interest picked up. On the one hand, new sources of energy became desirable; on the other, petroleum companies had large cash reserves that could be used for developing alternative energy sources. Private-sector interest in synthetic fuels was supported by increased federal funds for research, development, and demonstration. These were first supplied by the Energy Research and Development Administration (ERDA), later by the Department of Energy (DOE). Thus, when the public policy debate

---

AUTHOR'S NOTE: The material in this chapter is largely based on an article I wrote with Allen Kaufman, "Why It Is Difficult to Implement Industrial Policies: Lessons From the Synfuels Experience," *California Management Review* (Summer 1986), Volume 28, 98-115. © 1986 by The Regents of the University of California. Reprinted by permission of the Regents.

on synthetic fuels reemerged in earnest in 1979 as a result of the second energy crisis, induced by the Iranian Revolution, there were numerous public and private actors on the scene who had long favored legislation to commercialize synfuels (Kaufman, 1984).

Policy Development

The Carter administration introduced its synfuels program with much fanfare (Marcus & Kaufman, 1986). Declaring the "moral equivalent of war," it proposed to spend some $88 billion dollars in the 1980s to speed the development of synthetic fuels (Hershey, 1980). The initial proposal called for raising money through taxes on oil company windfall profits for a program to be administered by a private corporation later called the Synthetic Fuels Corporation (SFC). Chartered and financed by the federal government, the corporation would be given the freedom to invest its capital. It would be the nation's wealthiest corporation, with assets more than twice those of Exxon (Rosenbaum, 1987). Its goal would be to create the equivalent of 2.5 million barrels of oil daily by 1990, at a total price of $200-$400 billion.

The debate about the Carter program did not center on whether synfuels development was desirable, but on the scale of the program and what type of incentives would be most effective. Many critics cautioned against a massive crash effort and favored a more modest approach. Two basic positions emerged. The first, associated with Carter, called for the crash program to produce 500,000 barrels per day of crude-oil-equivalent (boed) by 1984 to meet military needs and an additional 2 million boed by 1989 to significantly reduce the amount of oil imported. Those production targets would require about 51 synfuels plants. To ensure the participation of enough firms to meet these goals, the crash program proposed numerous incentives, including price supports, direct subsidies, tax credits, and loan guarantees. Opponents to this plan sought more modest legislation. Instead of 50 or more plants over the next 20 years, supporters of a phased approach (e.g., the Senate Committee on Banking, Housing and Urban Affairs) called for 6 to 12 plants and a limited number of loan guarantees (Kaufman, 1984).

The integrated oil producers aligned themselves with either the crash or phased proposals in ways that aimed at promoting their competitive advantage. The industry was divided between firms that were vertically integrated and other firms (mostly independent oil producers) that were not. Among the integrated firms, the 8 top producers had somewhat different interests from those of the lesser forty or so integrated producers. The cost of raising capital for a synfuel plant, which might run $1-$3 billion, was not prohibitive for the top integrated firms. Their biggest need was for tax relief, not loan guarantees. They, therefore, objected to loan guarantees that would lower entry barriers and aid their competitors. Consequently, the top integrated producers—with the exception of ARCO—favored the phased program. Understandably, the lesser integrated producers—with the exception of Union Oil—lobbied for the crash program, or at least, for extensive loan guarantees so that they could secure financial resources to enter the emerging industry.

In contrast, the nonintegrated, independent oil producers did not debate the comparative virtues of the various types of incentives. They objected completely to the government's involvement in synfuels commercialization. Their main trade association, the Independent Petroleum Producers Association of America, denounced the synfuels efforts as a transferring of wealth from the independent producers to the integrated companies, as it appeared at the time that the windfall profits tax proposed by President Carter to fund government subsidies for the industry would come primarily from the independents.

In its final form, the Energy Security Act of 1980 (ESA) more closely approximated the crash program than the phased program. It favored the lesser integrated firms over the top majors or the independents. At the heart of the legislation was the SFC, which was to function as a publicly owned private enterprise governed by a seven-member board until 1992, when it would be terminated.

Constraints

Accompanying the government proposals to offer incentives for synfuel development were constraints, many of which were a legacy of the 1970s and were associated with environmental and other types of regulation. These constraints were especially important, because to justify investment in synfuels, the world price of oil in real terms would have had to nearly double from its 1980 level. Given this fact, a sponsor of a synthetic fuel project faced the possibility that price controls, environmental constraints, permit delays, and court actions could radically change the economics of a project. An example was the energy industry's concern about future energy rate regulation (Johnson, 1981). Companies were reluctant to invest because the future return might not justify the large risks. They were unwilling to take the downside risks, because they perceived a probable government floor on their upside potential (Nulty, 1980).

Another impediment resulted from environmental policies. For example, would standards be promulgated only after plants became operational or would these standards be known in advance? Whether the plants would need retrofitting after they were in use affected estimates of project costs and expected profitability. With uncertainty, it was difficult for companies to determine if they should proceed with specific projects. Environmental regulations had come into being that had not existed 10, 20, or 30 years previously, and the configuration of environmental regulations that would be enforced in the future was unknown.

Antitrust regulation created additional uncertainty. A synthetic fuel producer needed access to raw materials, the ability to transport the raw materials to a production facility, basic production capacity, and the ability to transport and market the fuels produced. Few companies were able to carry out all these functions. Most would prefer to share the risks by entering into joint ventures with other concerns. At a minimum, an integrated oil and gas company would supply the site, a part of the market, and the capital equipment; an engineering company would provide the know-how and management services. Such joint ventures, however, would be closely scrutinized under Section 7 of the Clayton Act as to their effects on competition.

These regulatory uncertainties made it extremely difficult for companies to plan. Instead of a willingness to invest, there was hesitation because of the unknown impact of government policies on future income. Firms were unable to accurately assess risk and opportunity and thus make the tradeoffs necessary for investment (Marcus, 1984; Marcus & Kaufman, 1986). In 1979, the Carter administration proposed that an Energy Mobilization Board (EMB) be created to deal with the regulatory uncertainties associated with synfuels development. The board would have three members appointed by the president and approved by Congress, and its purpose would be to "cut through the red tape, the delays, and the endless road block" caused by regulatory requirements (Hershey, 1983). EMB members, under the president's plan, would have designated up to 75 projects for fast-track regulatory consideration. They would have had the authority to draw up project decision schedules; set deadlines by which federal, state, and local agencies would have to accept or reject projects; and enforce schedules by stepping in and making a ruling whenever an agency failed to meet a deadline.

Disputes about the EMB's authority focused on its right to override substantive laws when they caused delays in licensing and construction. The White House did not want EMB to have such broad authority, but only the power to waive so-called procedural delays after a project had received all necessary approval and construction had begun. When the new legislation was being written, however, administration lobbyists made a different argument. They endorsed a sweeping waiver provision drafted for the House by Representative John Dingell (Democrat, Michigan) giving EMB power to override any law standing in the way of projects on the fast track. Congress ultimately rejected the proposal, but it did endorse a synfuels development corporation and promised to give the corporation approximately $88 billion in the long term, although it appropriated only $20 billion in the short term.

Enthusiasm Dissipated

Even during the Carter administration, the program to produce 2 million boed by 1992 got off to a slow start although the lure of incentives did touch off an "industrial gold rush" (Corrigan, 1979). Business interests converged on DOE with questions about how to get federal aid. Synfuels were described as "one of the biggest investment prospects in the 1980s," and major investment firms, such as Merrill Lynch, set up special synfuels groups and hired "energy experts" to concentrate on synfuels development. The construction and oil and gas companies that were already in the synfuels industry or that planned to enter formed a trade association, the Council on Synthetic Fuels, designed to help its members take advantage of the new incentives the government was offering.

All this activity took place despite "dire warnings" from experts that the appropriate means for carrying out a program of this scale were not available. Critics contended that so much energy would be required to produce synfuels that the net production of energy would be negative (Nulty, 1980). The Congressional Office of Technology Assessment warned that the goal of producing 500,000 boed entailed significant technological, economic, environmental, and social risks. It claimed the results were not worth the benefits and would create serious socioeconomic dislocation. A former deputy secretary of DOE, Jack O'Leary, predicted that environmentalists would disrupt synfuel development "faster than they did the nuclear industry" (Nulty, 1980). The financial community also expressed reservations, feeling that its involvement could turn corporations into entities whose profits would be affected in a major way by government dictates. From a stock evaluation point of view, these companies would command lower price earnings than corporations that were freer to compete to earn maximum profits.

There was a general agreement that the obstacles to creating a 2-million-boed industry by the end of the century were formidable. Assuming, conservatively, that it would take 6 years to complete a plant, a new project would have to get under way every 2 or 3 months from 1981 to 1986, and this timetable did not take into account possible permitting delays associated with environmental impact statements. A construction campaign to create a 2-million-boed industry by the end of the century would require 153,000 new technical workers and engineers. Where these workers would be found was not clear.

There were also arguments about the additional "red tape" imposed by the government program. Conoco applied for a $4 million grant for a feasibility study for a coal gasification plant, but after a long administrative proceeding, the government refused to grant the money. Construction costs were rising by $20,000 to $30,000 per hour, which added $6 million to the costs of a project every 2 weeks. If Conoco had proceeded to build a coal gasification plant, the delay would have cost the company nearly $100 million a year in interest.

Congress implied that it wanted the SFC to work mainly with companies that were *not* experienced energy producers. The motive was partly political, because Congress did not want to appear to be subsidizing the large integrated companies. The corporation's charter provided that its assistance could "not compete with or supplant" private investment available on reasonable terms. Many observers interpreted this to mean that companies with huge cash flows, such as the large integrated companies, could not seek assistance. These companies—who, some argued, had the know-how to produce synfuels—had to pursue projects on their own without government assistance (U.S. Congress, House Committee on Energy and Commerce, 1982, p. 16).

Regardless of what Congress implied, some of the large integrated companies sought government assistance. Some, such as Gulf, even managed to obtain this assistance. As a partner in an international venture, Gulf was eligible to participate in the building of a synfuel plant near Morgantown, West Virginia. Most of the companies that received federal funds, however, were not the large petroleum companies. The Great Plains coal gasification project, for example, was a joint venture by gas pipeline companies. The engineering firm W. R. Grace was involved in a feasibility study to produce methyl alcohol from coal. Union Carbide received funds to design a plant to produce minimum-Btu gas. Most companies, however, never got beyond the stage of feeling out the situation. They were not sure whether they wanted to be involved and what the risks and the likely consequences were if they did become involved.

The SFC's performance during the Reagan administration disappointed both phased and crash program proponents. As of January 1984, the SFC had made only two financial awards, for a total of $520 million to projects that promised to produce about 15,000 boed by 1985. These figures were obviously way below the original 500,000 boed by 1987 prescribed in the Energy Security Act. No doubt, economic circumstances contributed to the SFC's poor performance. Corporate enthusiasm for synfuels evaporated by 1981 as the world economy tumbled into its worst recession since the 1930s. As demand for oil dwindled, the energy companies unexpectedly discovered that oil was in oversupply—at least in the short run—and the price for a barrel of oil fell from $35 in 1980 to $29 in 1984. With projected profitability for synfuels based on oil prices of $40 to $70 a barrel, many firms canceled projects either scheduled for, or already under, construction. By 1982, over half the sponsors for SFC funding under its first solicitation had rescinded their applications (U.S. Congress, House Committee on Energy and Commerce, 1982, p. 16).

By the end of 1982, non-OPEC oil production had increased, world economic growth had stalled, and demand for energy had been significantly reduced. It was now apparent that the price of energy would not increase at a pace faster than the rate of inflation. As a consequence, numerous alternative fuels projects were abandoned. Furthermore, predictions abounded that high-quality coal gas would not be needed in the future because of major new discoveries of natural gas; 1980 was the first year since 1965 that the United States added more natural gas reserves than it consumed. It appeared that fast-rising prices and improved drilling techniques were likely to ensure even more discoveries in the immediate future.

Although these economic and supply changes help account for the lack of synfuel development, they cannot entirely explain SFC's failure. The SFC's designers had intended this semipublic bank as a corrective for market fluctuations to encourage corporate investment no matter what changes occurred in energy prices or the business cycle. But supporters of the SFC were not able to get public officials to wait out the business cycle changes, because divisions within both the business community and government paralyzed the program.

The dismantling of the SFC occurred during the Reagan administration. President Reagan's effective embrace of diverse elements of the business community is illustrated by the energy team that was appointed after the 1980 election. Although the team members cooperated in writing an energy report, substantive differences among opposing interests in the oil industry reemerged over implementation of the team's recommendations. Among the issues where differences were most strongly felt was synthetic fuels.

On entering office, Reagan's director of Management and Budget, David Stockman, recommended SFC's immediate dismantlement. Stockman had been an articulate spokesperson against subsidies to any sector of the energy industry, including conservation and solar as well as synfuels. The administration could not directly act against the SFC, however, because the SFC had wide and powerful support (Corrigan, 1983). Congress remained devoted because the SFC promised energy security to the nation and subsidies to home districts. Support ran deep in the Republican party, even among fiscal conservatives and free market supporters. Support also penetrated deeply into the business community. Union Oil, Exxon, Bechtel, and Fluor, even though they differed about what type of incentives were appropriate, still supported synfuels; many of these firms had shared their top executives with Reagan's Campaign Executive Business Advisory Committee, and none accepted Stockman's recommendation to completely eliminate the SFC.

Constrained by these interests, the administration moved against the SFC administratively. By rejecting Carter's SFC board in its entirety and delaying new appointments, Reagan undid whatever progress had been made under Carter (Plattner, 1983). Reagan did nominate a director for the seven-member board in May 1981, but a quorum for working meetings had to wait until September. And it was not until August 1982 that the board had its first full meeting. Reagan chose as chairman Edward Noble, whose business interests and political activities made him the ideal candidate to constrain the SFC. As a director of Noble

Affiliates, an independent Oklahoma energy company with revenues of about $200 million in oil and gas exploration, contract drilling, and heavy trucking, Noble represented the sector of the oil industry that most vehemently opposed ESA. The proverbial fox had gained access to the chicken coop.

With a quorum at last in September 1981, Noble attempted to shorten the corporation's life by calling for its termination in 1984. As the battle over the SFC's continued existence proceeded, confusion and demoralization set in among the corporation's personnel. Communication broke down between the staff and the board, between the staff and senior management, and between senior management and the board. These managerial problems left those who still supported synfuels distraught with the SFC's performance. Nor could the problems have come at a worse time, as they cost the SFC the opportunity to establish the industry before oil prices declined. After prices went down, management failures made it impossible to recover the opportunity to move forward ("Synfuel baby is thrown out," 1981). Nonetheless, SFC's resignation to the unfavorable market appraisal for synfuels investments did not escape criticism from some elements in the business community. The Committee for Economic Development continued its early and important advocacy of synfuels as it watched with alarm how the SFC gave way to political machinations and market fluctuations. The American Petroleum Institute persisted in its support of a public/private synfuels initiative, and the National Council for Synthetic Fuels vigorously expressed its opposition to Noble's subversion.

By December 1982, Congress stepped in. The Senate Appropriations Subcommittee on the Interior held oversight hearings on the SFC and demanded an end to the board's "sabotage" (Marcus & Kaufman, 1986). Building on these investigations, another Senate subcommittee, Oversight of Government Management, explored the board's performance and the ethical conduct of its members (Marcus & Kaufman, 1986). In response, the board tried to set priorities, simplify application procedures, and offer more attractive financial incentives. It reversed its initial intransigence and committed funds for synfuels projects.

This change in policy can be explained partially by congressional scrutiny and partially by the commitment of some board members to a strong synfuels program. Robert Monks, a Harvard-trained lawyer, resident of Maine, and an activist in liberal Republican politics, led the opposition. He believed that the SFC was not only an important agent for resolving the energy crisis, but also a promising experiment in the business-government cooperation he thought necessary if the United States was to meet the competitive challenges of the 1980s. In effect, Monks supported the SFC as an experiment in industrial policy.

But the board's image was tarnished again when two members resigned under charges of impropriety. By spring 1984, only two board members were left; three more had resigned citing personal reasons. The SFC had virtually self-destructed, but it may have been doomed anyway by its own mismanagement, the perceived oil glut, the displacement of energy by budget deficits as the central threat to national well-being, and the Reagan administration's commitment to remove distortions from the economy and keep the federal government out of programs unless it was absolutely necessary for the government to be involved.

When the leaders of the industrialized nations met for an international economic summit in 1984 it was the U.S. deficit, not energy, that commanded their attention. When Reagan arrived in London to attend the summit meeting, he demonstrated good faith to the allies by putting before them a budget package ratified by the Senate that would put a down payment on the deficit (Kilburn, 1984). Senate approval for this budget was won at the expense of the synfuels program. Republican dissidents in the Senate refused to accept any more cuts in social programs while the President remained unmoved by exhortations to lower defense spending. The stalemate was broken by the transfer $2 billion from the SFC to nondefense spending programs (Tale, 1984).

Limits on Interventionist Policies

The case of synfuels shows that the ability to carry out strongly interventionist, long-term energy policies in the United States is severely limited. Centrally directed development efforts, such as the synfuels program, often go awry. Their goals are not achieved. In the case of synfuels, the government provided incentives for development, but failed to remove barriers. Business interests responded to the synfuels opportunity in a hesitant, uncertain, and inconsistent manner. Conflict in the business community stood in the way of progress. Ultimately, the whole program, which was hastily constructed in an atmosphere of crisis, unraveled. It was put on hold, without prospect for much attention unless the country again faced a critical energy shortage.

The factors that led to the demise of the synfuels program are likely to affect any long-term, sector-specific energy policy. They include:

- Rapid changes in market forces—Government sensitivity to sudden shifts in supply and demand makes it difficult to carry out consistent long-term policies. In the case of synfuels, the perception of a supply problem inspired support for stepped-up government intervention, but subsequent rapid changes in market forces left the synfuels program languishing.
- Intragovernmental politics—An inability to resolve differences between government programs designed to promote and control development is likely to hinder progress. The contradictory character of government signals to the private sector creates uncertainty and leads to business hesitancy in making long-term or large capital commitments.
- Business politics—Contention among firms is likely to stand in the way of making gains. In the synfuels case, the outright opposition of the independent oil producers and the lukewarm support of the large integrated producers left the program without a strong constituency once national concern over the energy issue had subsided. Interfuel politics also played a role, as environmental activists were committed to conservation and solar power and did their part in dampening enthusiasm for the program.
- Design problems—Programs announced by politicians in the heat of a crisis are likely to be too ambitious and exceed the capacity of the government or the private sector to accomplish objectives. Grandiose claims by the Carter administration about what the synfuels program was supposed to accomplish diminished its credibility and made it an easy target for critics.

The systematic pursuit of long-term energy policies is unlikely unless a crisis lasts long enough to mobilize a large segment of the population (as, for example, with U.S. defense policy in the postwar period). At the same time, an economy in which adversary relations between sectors prevails is likely to abandon white elephants more readily than more centralized systems. With a diversity of interests, some participants become watchdogs for values that are neglected by others. The system is thus likely to rapidly alter its behavior in response to changes in the external situation and to correct errors as it proceeds.

Although heightened conflict mitigates errors, it also may create them by allocating resources according to political, not economic criteria. In the synfuels case, government intervention was poorly executed *and* misconceived, as the energy crisis ultimately did not require such extensive government intervention for its solution. Heightened tension did not prevent the synfuels "error" from coming into being, but played a role in aborting the program before it developed into a white elephant that might have plagued the nation for many generations to come. In a more centralized system, even if intended policies are "wrong," the government may go ahead and pursue them. At the same time, if intended policies are "right," in an adversary system they face a severe test. Heightened conflict may offer the promise of aborting poorly conceived policies, but the question remains: Does a system where conflict is common have the capacity to implement "correctly" conceived policies?

7

Nuclear Power

In this chapter, I turn to nuclear power, first tracing its history (Rolph, 1979), and in the next chapter continuing the story with a discussion of the role of nuclear power in the future of the electric utility industry. The history of nuclear power is in many ways similar to the history of synfuels. In both instances a combination of government and market inducements and limitations simultaneously acted to promote and then stifle development. Although economic theory asserts that technological innovation and the substitution of one energy production system for another should take place as prices rise and instabilities occur, the realities of the process of substitution are rarely smooth or instantaneous. To move from reliance on one system of energy production to another is a difficult and uncertain process whose outcome is highly indefinite. The unanticipated obstacles that have arisen in cost and safety to the "peaceful uses of the atom" should yield caution when considering the government role in energy development.

Origins and Development

The Atomic Energy Commission (AEC) was established in 1946 with the primary purpose of weapons development. Glenn Seaborg, codiscoverer of the element plutonium and chairman of the AEC from 1961 to 1971, when it licensed the first nuclear power plants, was an enthusiastic supporter of the civilian uses of nuclear energy. Along with other scientists—and much fanfare from the media—he worked to establish a large civilian nuclear power program. From the beginning, however, his vision of atomic-powered plenty was not shared by all scientists. A Manhattan Project task force appointed after the war concluded that the "production of power for ordinary commercial use does not appear economically sound nor advisable" (quoted in Ford, 1982, p. 29). A draft report on the prospects for nuclear power prepared by J. Robert Oppenheimer for David Lilienthal, first head of the AEC, was also extremely pessimistic, and private industry was reluctant to invest money for the development of a commercial industry.

It was actually in a relatively small office within the AEC, the Naval Reactors Branch, under the leadership of Hyman Rickover, that substantial progress on the design of what was to become the first commercial reactor—the pressurized water reactor—was made. Rickover's aim was to produce the first nuclear-powered submarine, one that could travel at high speeds and remain submerged for long periods of time. Rickover brought together Alvin Weinberg's design for a nuclear power reactor (Weinberg was the head of the government's Oak Ridge Laboratory) with the engineering of the Westinghouse Corporation, the testing capabilities of AEC's remote laboratory in Idaho, and his own managerial genius to produce the first nuclear-powered submarine, the *Nautilus,* in record time.

In anticipation of Rickover's triumph, President Eisenhower made his famous atoms for peace speech in December 1953 and launched the civilian nuclear power program. In August of the next year, Congress passed an amended Atomic Energy Act. Rather than having the government produce atomic energy and sell it to the public, the Republican administration insisted that the AEC issue licenses to private utilities to own and operate commercial nuclear power stations. To carry out this mission the AEC could pass any regulations it deemed necessary "to protect the health and safety of the public."

During hearings on the proposed legislation, the Joint Committee on Atomic Energy (JCAE) was told by Edward Teller, father of the hydrogen bomb, that accidents were possible. Fatalities could be numerous and large quantities of poison could be released into the environment. Teller, therefore, advocated siting reactors as far as possible from human populations. Other prominent scientists, such as James Conant, expressed reservations about the desirability of a large-scale nuclear power program. Industry representatives, concerned about possible liability in the event of an accident, asked for further study. The Brookhaven National Laboratory produced what became known as "WASH-740": In a worst case, 3400 people would die and another 43,000 would be injured (Ford, 1982). Concerned, Congress passed the Price Anderson Act, which guaranteed that in the event of an accident individual companies would not be liable. The AEC would organize an insurance fund to compensate the victims.

The Advisory Committee on Reactor Safeguards (ACRS), originally called the Reactor Safeguards Committee, had been established in 1947 to advise AEC managers (Okrent, 1982). Composed of 15 eminent scientists, from 1947 to 1953 it was chaired by Teller. Teller recalled that it was viewed as being "as popular" and "as necessary—as a traffic cop"; it was referred to as the Committee for Reactor Prevention or the Brake Department by some nuclear power officials (Ford, 1982, p. 51). The ACRS came to play an important, although far from decisive, role in the licensing process, as utilities sought first a construction permit and then an operating permit. At both stages, the ACRS conducts a review in which it examines the proposed plant's safety and its effect on the environment (Wood, 1983). Decisions, which can be appealed to a special panel, the commission, and the courts, are actually made by the Atomic Safety and Licensing Board Panel, a three-person panel made up of a lawyer and two scientists.

The ACRS first came into sharp conflict with the AEC over the AEC's 1955 decision to grant a license to a consortium of utilities to build a demonstration breeder reactor, called Fermi, on the shores of Lake Erie midway between Detroit and Toledo. The United Auto Workers brought suit against the AEC to prevent construction, but the Supreme Court ruled in 1961 that AEC had the right to proceed. Congress had delegated to the commission the authority to license nuclear facilities, and it had the discretion to use this authority as it saw fit. The Fermi incident was significant in that it was the first long licensing delay, though typical of the controversies that became common in later years. It also laid the groundwork for future controversy. In response to the dispute, the JCAE held hearings and Congress made two significant changes in the licensing process. First, it gave the ACRS formal statutory existence and specific review responsibilities for licensing applications. Second, it required a mandatory public hearing for every application.

Scaling Up

The major question about conventional nuclear power reactors in the early 1960s was their economic feasibility. Cost overruns and delays had plagued the demonstration plants at Shippingport, Dresden, and Indian Point. AEC estimates were that nuclear power was 30% to 60% more expensive than electricity generated from conventional power sources. General Electric and Westinghouse campaigns to sell nuclear power were based on the premise that economies of scale would eliminate this cost differential. Early reactors averaged about 150 MW generating capacity. In 1963, General Electric sold General Public Utilities the first 515 MW plant at Oyster Creek, New Jersey. Both Westinghouse and General Electric began plans for reactors in the range of 800-1100 MW. To protect populations in nearby areas, engineering safeguards such as containment buildings were added.

A major concern was the possibility of a pipe rupture or other major blockage of the cooling system that could lead to overheating in the reactor core. An update of WASH 740 was carried out by scientists at Brookhaven, who found that a major accident with a 1000 MW plant could produce as many as 45,000 fatalities. One shortcoming of the study was that the probability of an accident of that consequence occurring was not calculated. Efforts to carry out such calculations were difficult because the complexity of nuclear power plants meant that a seemingly small and inconsequential event might develop into a major mishap. Moreover, the results of the WASH-740 update were not made public because intervenors might have used the findings to block construction of additional nuclear power plants (Ford, 1982). Members of the ACRS expressed concerned about the bolts that held the larger reactors in place and the reliability of the control rod system, but what was perhaps their strongest criticism was reserved for the emergency core cooling system (ECCS). The ECCS might not function properly in the event of an emergency.

The JCAE appointed a task force headed by the Oak Ridge National Laboratory scientist and former ACRS member W. K. Ergen to study the problem. Simulations at the AEC National Reactor Testing Station in Idaho showed that in the event of a loss-of-coolant accident the fuel in the reactor would get hotter faster than previously believed. There would be insufficient flow of the emergency core cooling water to the reactor core. Morris Rosen, head of the Division of Reactor Standards in 1971 and regulator staff liaison with the ACRS, wrote in a 1971 memo that the performance of the ECCS could not "be defined with sufficient assurance to provide a clear basis for licensing" (Ford, 1982, p. 108). The AEC did not want ECCS design to become a point of contention at each individual licensing hearing. It therefore decided to issue a generic rule approving the design, but to do so, had to hold public hearings. These hearings were the first major public hearings the commission held on the general issue of reactor safety, and they expanded into one of the longest and most complex the government ever has held, lasting for almost 2 years and resulting in nearly 50,000 pages of testimony. In December 1973, the AEC adopted stringent ECCS standards (Del Sesto, 1982). Operating plants had to shut down until they complied with the standards, and extensive retrofitting was required in many instances. Moreover, applicants for new construction permits were forced to redesign their plants.

At about the same time, the courts took up a case that had to do with the effort of an environmental group to stop construction of a nuclear power plant on the Chesapeake Bay because of the threat of thermal pollution. The environmental group maintained that the AEC had acted in violation of the National Environmental Policy Act (NEPA) because it had not issued an Environmental Impact Statement (EIS). Judge James Skelly Wright ruled that construction of the Calvert Cliffs plant and all others would have to be halted while environmental impact statements were prepared.

In July 1971 James Schlesinger replaced Glenn Seaborg as head of the AEC and launched a new study to determine the risks of nuclear power. Norman Rasmussen of the MIT Nuclear Engineering Department was named study director. The methodology, borrowed from the Apollo space program, was to be fault-tree analysis, with the basic idea of analyzing the individual faults that were possible and combining them to produce accident sequences. Then data on the probability of the individual faults could be combined and the overall probability that an accident sequence would occur could be computed.

The problems with this methodology were well known. Hardware failures could be modeled, but not design deficiencies that might be complicated by human error. Fault-tree analysis depended on engineering judgment, and engineers often lacked the imagination to consider relevant possibilities or assign correct probabilities. Twenty to 35% of the failures that occurred during the Apollo program had not been correctly identified by fault-tree analysis.

The reactor safety study used two model plants as data sources—plants that were not necessarily representative of conditions generally prevalent in the industry. Moreover, the study relied on the blueprints for these plants and did not take into account discrepancies between drawings and actual conditions that might come into being because of quality control problems. The working draft of the Rasmussen report released in the summer of 1974 was severely criticized for not adequately considering common-mode failures—failures that occurred when a single event simultaneously incapacitated redundant safety systems. It was argued that the Rasmussen investigators failed to take into account the possible effects of fires, which could be "severe and widespread," or "consider the possibility of accident conditions in the plant leading to panic in the crew with subsequent abandonment" (Ford, 1982, p. 161).

In an effort to restore confidence in the nuclear power program, Congress changed the ground rules for regulation. It separated the AEC regulatory and promotional functions in the Nuclear Regulatory Commission (NRC) and the Energy Research and Development Administration (ERDA). Subsequently, in 1977, ERDA was incorporated into the newly created Department of Energy (DOE). The JCAE also was stripped of some of its authority and in 1976 was eliminated.

Between 1969 and 1974 it took an average of 67 months to move from construction permit to full power license. In the period 1975-1980 this figure jumped to 106 months. The elapsed time between a safety analysis report, one of the initial steps in licensing, and full-power operation increased by more than 200% between 1960 and 1980. Although many factors complicated the situation, including high interest and inflation rates, construction problems, and decreased demand for electricity, there can be little doubt that protracted and complex licensing procedures and regulatory measures associated with technical uncertainty added to the costs of nuclear power. In many cases final costs exceeded initial estimates by more than 100%. The average cost of electricity per kilowatt at a completed plant in 1971 was $150. By 1977, this cost had increased to more than $500. Economics of scale had not played a role in lowering the costs of nuclear power. To the contrary, as more plants were built and they grew in size and complexity, technical uncertainty surrounding nuclear power increased, regulatory requirements became more stringent and cumbersome, and the costs escalated to the point where nuclear power was even less competitive with alternative means for generating electricity than it had been at the outset.

From Technical Issues to Human Factors

Initial questions about nuclear power focused on technical issues (for example, the ECCS controversy); the questions raised were about the design of nuclear power plants. But as actual operating experience began to accumulate, the major issue became whether any design, no matter how good, could be implemented adequately. A perfect engineering design required care and diligence by numerous workers with different backgrounds, expertise, and levels of authority. The coordination of this activity rested with individual utilities, which had to adopt sensible operating procedures and make sure that employees carried out procedures as written. What if worker sabotage occurred? What if the industry mechanisms for policing itself—the reactor safety committees that were supposed to function as self-regulatory mechanisms at each plant—broke down? These types of questions were increasingly raised in the period prior to the incident at Three Mile Island (TMI).

Prior to the incident at TMI, there had been numerous warnings about managerial problems. A number of reports were published that raised issues of organization and administration (see Kim, 1982). In 1975, NRC staff memeber Stephen Hanauer wrote a memo on "important" safety issues facing the commission in which he emphasized the role that human errors could play in leading to major accidents. "Present designs do not make adequate provision for the limitations of people," he stressed (Ford, 1982, p. 216). Hanauer was concerned that a small crew of operators with no more than high school education would be relied on in the event of an emergency. Another issue Hanauer raised was that incident reports repeatedly showed that vital valves had a tendency to malfunction. This information was not being fed back to key industry personnel. Hanauer advised that means be found to improve worker performance and "to improve the design of equipment so that it is less dependent on human performance."

At JCAE hearings in 1976, three General Electric executives testified about problems in procedures and staffing. In December 1978, the ACRS, in a study released just 4 months before the TMI incident, emphasized that inadequacies in procedures and staffing were causing numerous human-related errors. The ACRS report asserted that up to 50% of all incidents were the result of human failures, including reliance on inadequate instructions, procedures, and guides; a lack of attention to human/machine interfaces; and improperly trained personnel. The ACRS argued that analysis and evaluation of incident reports should be more fully utilized and that "although many of the reported events are not particularly significant individually, . . . in the aggregate, they may be indicators of more serious events" (Sommers, 1984).

The Post-TMI Consensus

Although awareness of deficiencies in the human aspect of nuclear power plant management was common prior to the TMI incident, uncertainty about the safety of nuclear power plants did not move from a concern about the technical aspects of nuclear power to a concern about the human aspects until after the accident. So numerous were the reports prepared after the TMI incident that it was called "the most studied nuclear accident in history" (U.S. General Accounting Office, 1980). On April 20, 1979, the NRC began its first formal investigation. Carried out by the Office of Inspection and Enforcement and completed in August, it confirmed inadequacies in organizational and administration including operator training and performance, information flow, and accident analysis. Later studies (Kemeny, 1979; Rogovin, 1980; U.S. Congress, House Committee on Interior and Insular Affairs, 1979; U.S. Congress, Senate Committee on Environment and Public Works, Subcommittee on Nuclear Regulation, 1980a, 1980b; U.S. Nuclear Regulatory Commission, Office of Inspection and Enforcement, 1979, Office of Nuclear Reactor Regulation, 1979) found that the primary deficiency was inadequate attention to the human element. Fundamental changes in several aspects of nuclear power administration and organization were suggested, including increased management commitment, better training, greater operator qualification, added preparation for the unusual, and better feedback of information.

On April 11, 1979, President Carter established a 12-person commission and charged it with conducting a comprehensive study and investigation of the incident; John Kemeny, president of Dartmouth College, was appointed chairman. The Kemeny report, published in October 1979, found that the "fundamental problems" were "people-related" not equipment related. Key issues were "structural problems in the various organizations, . . . deficiencies in various processes, and . . . lack of communication among . . . officials and groups." There was a "mindset" focusing on "the safety of the equipment," which resulted in downplaying of the "human element." NRC and the utilities "failed to recognize sufficiently that . . . human beings . . . manage and operate the plants [and] constitute an important safety system." According to the Kemeny commission, factors that contributed to the confusion included failure to learn lessons from previous incidents. Divided responsibility among the utility, its parent company, the reactor supplier, the architect engineer, and the NRC was cited as a reason for this shortcoming. The commission concluded that the implications of a similar incident at the Davis-Bessie plant had not been learned and applied by TMI personnel. Management had failed to acquire sufficient information about other safety problems, failed to analyze adequately information they obtained, and failed to act on what they did know.

In June 1979, the NRC entered into a contract with the Washington law firm of Rogovin, Stern, and Hage to direct a special inquiry into the TMI incident. NRC staff, technical consultants, and the national laboratories played a major role in this study, which was published in four volumes in January 1980. The main conclusion again was that the TMI accident was not a "hardware problem" but a "management problem" stemming from factors such as lack of coordination of responsibility among utilities, designers, and manufacturers. The investigators recommended "systematic evaluation of operating experience," strengthening of on-site technical and management capability, and "greater application of human factors engineering." The NRC was advised to establish an expanded Financial Analysis Office to "monitor situations in which business considerations may impact on nuclear safety." The Rogovin report also noted that incidents very similar to that at TMI happened before, but the implications of these incidents had not been understood by TMI operators and analyses had not been effectively communicated to utility personnel.

The Senate TMI investigation (U.S. Congress, Senate Committee on the Environment and Public Works, Subcommittee on Nuclear Regulations, 1980a, 1980b) noted that prior to the TMI incident, the NRC relied primarily on a "defense-in-depth" philosophy—"a focus on conservative design and operating margins and . . . redundancy of components and systems" to compensate for the fact that risks and uncertainties could not be reduced to "zero." But the accident revealed the fallacy of this approach. The Senate investigators criticized past methods of disseminating operation information as being "generally weak and unsystematic."

After reviewing the numerous reports, the NRC tried to ensure that "all TMI-related recommendations were considered" (U.S. Nuclear Regulatory Commission, 1980a, 1980b, 1982). It prioritized the recommendations according to the "best judgment" of NRC managers and technical groups, using a quantitative scoring system that was based on items like safety significance, type of improvement, NRC resource requirements, industry resource requirements, and timing. On this basis, 100 actions were selected for implementation. Kim (1982) analyzed the processes of "error correction" that the NRC undertook following the TMI incident and examined the bases for the action items. He found that the TMI Action Plan was comprehensive in that it took into account almost all the important deficiencies of the nuclear regulatory system reported by the various investigatory groups, but it was not "synoptic" in the sense of planning actions in detail in correspondence with a "deductive-rational" model. Most actions were ambiguously defined and the required resources given to carrying out these actions were only an approximation of what was actually needed. Moreover, Kim argued that the staff's judgment in task selection was accompanied by nothing more than the staff's sincerity and integrity. The staff did not represent the problem in terms of its casual structure or weigh the costs and benefits of options. It simply collected recommendations from the TMI investigations and classified them loosely according to subject matter and other criteria.

As Schon (1971) argued, often it is a crisis of some sort that brings ideas into "good currency," permitting ideas previously submerged or ignored to gain public notice and acceptance. A critical shift in the situation creates a demand for new ideas to explain, diagnose, and remedy the perceived crisis. Hard evidence associated with the crisis appears to refute old ideas. New ideas are then able to move from the margins to the mainstream. Such was the case with nuclear power as the idea of human factors moved from the periphery into a more central concern.

8

The Electric Utility Industry Faces the Future

Itself affected by changing national concerns such as economic growth, environmental quality, and energy, the electric power industry in turn influences the competitiveness of U.S. business, the quality of the natural environment, and energy availability (Fenn, 1983). The largest consumer of primary energy in the United States, the electric power industry consumes over one third of total U.S. energy demand. At the same time it supplies one tenth of that demand, losing 65% to 75% of the energy in conversion, transmission, and distribution. Neither a producer of energy like the oil companies nor a consumer like individual households, utilities convert energy from one form to another. The energy created is attractive because it is clean, versatile in its uses, and can be moved great distances nearly instantaneously. Demand for electricity has grown as a percentage of energy demand even as demand for energy as a whole has contracted; consumption of electricity grew from one quarter of total energy consumption in 1973 to about a third in 1990. The major participants in the industry are about 200 investor-owned utilities that generate 78% of the power and supply 76% of the customers. The industry is very capital intensive, heavily regulated, and has a large impact on other industries, including aluminum, steel, electronics, computers, and robotics. In this chapter I sketch the recent history of the electric utility industry in the United States and examine the growth and development of nuclear power production within the context of the industry.

New Pressures and Uncertainties

New pressures and uncertainties have had a profound impact on the economic viability of the electric power industry, forcing utility companies to reexamine numerous assumptions that previously governed their behavior. The main strategy the industry followed after World War II was to grow and build. During this period demand increased rapidly at a rate of over 7% per year. New construction yielded economies of scale, greater efficiencies, and declining marginal costs. Public utility commissions lowered prices, stimulating additional demand that the utilities were required by law to meet. As a regulated natural monopoly, they had an obligation to serve. As long as prices fell, demand continued to rise, and additional construction was necessary. Once the industry earned its allowed rate of return, the only way to increase profits was to expand the rate base by building new plants and equipment.

This idyllic period of industry growth came to an end in the 1970s. Numerous forces coalesced to force a reevaluation of the prior strategy. In brief the effect of these forces can be seen in the industry's deteriorating financial condition (Navarro, 1985):

1. Fuel prices escalated, including the weighted average costs of all fossil fuels (oil, coal, and natural gas) and the spot market price of uranium oxide.
2. Economic growth rates slowed.
3. Operating and maintenance costs, including the costs of labor, supplies and material, and administrative expenses went up, leading to higher costs per unit of capacity (kilowatt-hour, or kwh).
4. The price of electricity went up.
5. Sales growth rates declined.
6. Interest and inflation rates accelerated.
7. The cost of capital and the yield on bonds grew.
8. Construction costs rose.
9. Capital costs for nuclear- and coal-powered plants increased.

10. The average cost of new generating capacity and installed capacity per kwh went up.
11. Net earnings, earnings per share, and revenues per kwh went down, and long-term debt escalated.
12. New long-term bonds and stock had to be issued and short-term bank loans made.
13. Interest coverage ratios and credit ratings declined.
14. Surplus generating capacity increased.
15. Major generating units were canceled and capital appropriations cut back.

Antinuclear, proenvironmental, and proconsumer groups came into being. Formidable opponents of the utilities, they brought lawsuits under laws passed in the early 1970s like NEPA to block or delay construction projects. Public referenda were held and public participation in the planning process expanded. Socially concerned shareholders challenged construction of new nuclear power plants and other utility decisions. The number of proposals dealing with social responsibility made at annual meetings in the industry went up at the same time as Wall Street analysts' assessments and bond ratings went down. Government agencies imposed additional regulatory requirements. Environmental and safety regulations increased costs. EPA rules required that the utilities build stack gas scrubbers and cooling towers and that they use clean but low-quality coal. Large sums of money had to be spent on the purchase, operation, and maintenance of air and water pollution control equipment. NRC requirements affecting nuclear power plant operations, including operator training, emergency planning, security, and radiation protection, grew increasingly stringent, with new restrictions after the TMI accident. The industry complained that the government retroactively introduced the new requirements after construction on nuclear power plants had started.

The federal government affected utility operations in other ways. It banned the reprocessing of spent nuclear fuel, forcing the utilities to absorb the costs of long-term on-site storage. Energy regulations prohibited the construction of new, large oil-burning plants and discouraged the use of existing oil-burning plants. PURPA, passed in 1978, deregulated interstate power sales. Not only were wholesale power sales no longer subject to controls, but the utilities had to purchase power from qualifying facilities at fully avoided costs (Zardkoohi, 1986). In addition, public policymakers allowed imports of inexpensive hydropower from Canada.

Perhaps the greatest change took place in the electric power companies' relationship to the public utility commissions (Anderson, 1981). This once friendly relationship deteriorated under the onslaught of the other changes taking place. Pressure was felt to add citizen representation, create permanent public intervenors, and expand the role of state government in energy policy planning and decision making. The main issue that state and local commissions confronted was how to hold rate increases to a minimum in a period of generally rising prices when utility costs were growing and utility abilities to keep up with these escalating costs were shrinking. The industry argued that short-run rate suppression would only lead to higher costs in the long run, as the utilities would be unprepared to meet rising energy demand when economic recovery surely occurred. In a period of accelerating inflation, regulatory lag in granting rate relief could have serious repercussions. Many public utility commissions therefore granted the electric power companies' requests for automatic fuel adjustment clauses to allow the utilities, without further review, to pass fuel increases on to customers. The number of requests for rate increases grew as did the dollar amounts requested, but the percentage of rate increase requests granted actually went down. Many commissions also gave the utilities allowances for funds used during construction (AFUDC). AFUDC created paper earnings in that these noncash accounting entries credited net income with imputed returns on funds tied up in new construction. AFUDC became a component of utility earnings when actual internal cash flow per construction outlay was declining.

Other issues arose over lifeline rates and time-of-day pricing. Consumer groups favored the former for protecting the poor and other segments of the population vulnerable to sudden price hikes. Environmental groups favored the latter because it promoted conservation. Less obvious matters, such as accounting and depreciation issues, often determined the extent to which public utility commissions were friendly to industry interests. As the utilities' relationship with the commissions deteriorated, investment houses started to give poor ratings to the commissions.

Industry Responses

As the utilities' traditional grow-and-build strategy became increasingly untenable, different segments in the industry followed different courses, based on divergent perceptions of where the trends would lead and what the future would bring (Fenn, 1983).

Marketing Differentiation

Raising rates 10%-20% above the inflation rate might be self-defeating in the long run because it would affect demand. Also self-defeating in the long run might be advertising and other programs that moved away from promoting electricity use toward the promotion of conservation. More in line with utility interests were creative rate designs that promoted use when excess capacity was available and discouraged use when it was not available, and multiple rate structures for different classes of customers were also designed.

Cost Reduction

Almost all the utilities tried to negotiate long-term contracts with lower fuel procurement costs. They also tried to take advantage of opportunities for lower fuel costs on spot markets. Attempts were made to limit construction, maintenance, and administrative costs, but these attempts were not always successful. When all else failed, utilities broke with prevailing norms in the industry and laid off workers. The save-your-way-to-success strategy, however, had inherent limitations. Increasing cost pressures were intense. If a utility was lucky enough to have low-cost excess supply, one option was to sell it as wholesale power at discount rates to other utilities, thereby competing directly with cheap Canadian hydro.

Modified Grow-and-Build

A number of utilities pursued a modified grow-and-build strategy based on the assumption that economic growth would recover and conservation and renewable energy would not be able to handle the increased demand. These utilities continued their emphasis on nuclear power construction or shifted toward coal. They placed little emphasis on conservation or alternative energy sources. They voluntarily stretched out construction schedules or mothballed plants rather than abandoning them altogether.

Capital Minimization

By default more than design, some utilities with high reserve margins, no new construction, and cutbacks in construction spending pursued the option of capital minimization. With excess generating capacity and sluggish demand growth, they had little choice. These utilities might sell existing generating capacity. Any new generating facilities were established via joint ownership. These utilities initiated and joined regional generation and distribution pools and tended to introduce conservation programs to lower peak demand.

Renewable Energy Supply

In areas of rapidly growing energy demand where the regulatory climate discouraged nuclear and coal plant construction, utilities had no option but to explore alternative energy sources. In these utilities there was a relatively pronounced shift toward the use of renewable energy. They positioned themselves as contracting agents and energy brokers, shifting the risk for developing new capacity to third party developers. There was increasing use of outside entrepreneurs and reliance on the addition of small modular units of capacity. Small increments in capacity were added as needed in the form of wind, geothermal, fuel cells, hydro, biomass, cogeneration, conservation, and load management, providing the flexibility of short lead times in comparison to nuclear and coal construction.

Diversification

Diversification was attractive in that it freed utilities from the profit limitations imposed by the public utility commissions (Russo, 1989), in theory reducing business risk and making the companies more attractive to investors. Another attraction was the synergistic side benefits that diversification could have on the company's main line of business. Return on equity from the regulated portions of the business had long been stuck at about 11%, making the possibility of investing in fast-growing, more profitable ventures especially appealing. But which ventures should the electric power companies choose? The options ranged from oil and gas exploration to coal mining, energy engineering, engineering services, real estate, computer services, telecommunications, and fish hatcheries. From a theoretical and practical point of view, the question was why would a particular company choose one strategy over another, and what was the likely effect on its business and social performance, including nuclear power plant safety?

The Role of Nuclear Power

For the utilities, nuclear power's initial attraction was the maximization of capital investments (Ahearne, 1983). So long as the rate of return allowed by public utility commissions was fixed, the only way to increase profits was to expand the rate base. The need to expand the rate base existed in the 1960s when the demand for power was growing 7.3% per year. In a decade's time, this growth translated into the need to double existing generating capacity. The accepted wisdom in the industry was that cheaper power came from economies of scale. Nuclear power, being the most capital-intensive form of power generation, was surely the technology of choice. With the rise of fossil fuel prices following the 1973 oil embargo, the attraction of nuclear power only grew. In comparison to coal, the fuel costs were relatively low, about a third of the total costs of production as opposed to two thirds with coal. Nuclear power involved the substitution of capital, which amounted to two thirds of the generating costs, for a nonrenewable resource, coal, whose price was tied to oil. Moreover, with the ascendance of the environmental movement, nuclear power appeared at first to have an additional advantage: It was less polluting. It involved virtually no emissions of sulfur dioxide, carbon dioxide, or other pollutants into the atmosphere.

Between 1972 and 1974, the utilities ordered 79 new nuclear power plants. Thirteen of these orders came from utilities with no previous experience with nuclear power. Major problems developed, traceable to the financial pressures the utilities confronted in the postembargo period and the institutional relationships in the industry (Campbell, 1988).

The main advantage that nuclear power had over coal was fixed capital costs and low fuel costs. With nuclear, the initial costs of construction were great, but they yielded substantial operating benefits, although the unfortunate tail of waste disposal costs strung out indefinitely into the future. With coal, construction costs were modest, but the operating costs were high, primarily because of the expense of fuel.

The environmental damage was immediate. As long as the incentive for the utilities was to maximize capital, nuclear was more attractive than coal, and when fuel costs skyrocketed with the oil embargo, the advantages of nuclear seemed even greater. But for capital costs to be substituted for fuel costs, it was necessary that capital be available at a reasonable rate, and the capital costs of nuclear power got out of hand. With high energy prices after 1973, demand for power decreased to about half of what it was in the 1960s. Construction work continued, but while still incomplete, this construction work was not allowed to be included as part of the rate base. Only when a plant was actually producing power could it achieve this status. In the meantime, utility earnings were not sufficient to cover the cost of capital. Utilities could not use retained earnings to finance new nuclear power construction, because the retained earnings were controlled by public utility commissions that established price and profit limits. Retained earnings had to be small to demonstrate that the public utility commissions were carrying out their mandate to serve the public interest.

During the 1970s only about 60% of the rate increase requests that the utilities made were granted. The utilities applied for investments for construction work in progress to be included in the rate base, but consumers opposed such requests and the public utility commissions often denied them. With the cost of capital rising, the utilities' need for capital grew. To finance nuclear power construction, they had to tap capital markets. Inflation during this period was going up at unprecedented rates, and therefore the utilities had to offer lucrative interest rates on bonds to attract investors. As a consequence, their interest payments on outstanding debt increased. The interest coverage ratios (the relationship between annual earnings and annual interest payments on debt) rose, and their bond ratings declined. Utilities also sold new shares at low prices and raised dividend yields to attract investors. Their market-to-book ratios (the current selling price of stocks over total assets) declined, and price-to-earnings ratios slipped. With trouble raising new capital and financing nuclear power projects, utilities started to cancel projects. Only 13 new orders for nuclear power plants were placed between 1975 and 1978. All of these orders ultimately were canceled or were indefinitely postponed.

Another weakness of nuclear power in comparison to coal was that whereas coal had a long history, technologically nuclear was in its infancy. In 1979, the TMI nuclear accident shook the industry. It was followed by the second oil price shock, which was associated with the

Iranian Revolution. The world plunged into the worst recession since the Great Depression, and demand for power slipped as conservation took hold in response to higher energy prices and weakening economic conditions. After 1979, the utilities made no new orders for nuclear power plants and canceled construction even at sites where significant progress had been made.

Institutional Influences

The decline in nuclear power did not take place only because of the financial pressures. Institutional influences played a role (Thomas, 1988). In comparison with France, where nuclear power gained momentum, three differences were important. The first was that in the United States private competitive markets allocate most capital, whereas in France the state has greater control. Debt is not such a great burden on the French utility industry. The second factor was that in the United States the state has control over profit rates via public regulation, whereas in France, utilities are publicly owned. Electricity rates in France are not influenced by public utility commissions. Third, in France standardization of plants had offered many benefits. The nuclear power program has greater capacity to learn from experience. In the United States, the complexity of institutional arrangements prevents this unified approach.

Learning From Experience

Learning from experience is critical to the success of a nuclear power program. Feedback of design, production, and operational experience is one of the most important ways for progress to take place with respect to any technology, but was especially so with regard to nuclear power in the early years when it was relatively untried and untested. Nuclear designs were difficult to test, production costs were high, the number of operating units was few, and the safety implications of failure were great. Whole systems could not be subjected to destructive testing. Subsystems could be, but the effects on the whole system could be investigated only through computer simulation. Because subsystems were highly interdependent, simulation might miss the full consequences of failure. In the United States, with a small number of plants operating and little standardization, it was difficult to accumulate meaningful statistical analyses of plant performance (U.S. Congress, House

Committee on Energy and Commerce, 1988). Even when design changes were determined to be necessary, they might not be carried out because of regulatory delays and the expense of making unique changes on custom-built systems.

In France standardization reduced construction costs, prevented delays, and simplified repairs and maintenance. Efficiencies were achieved in the recognition and correction of error. When an error was discovered it had uniform applicability. Design improvements had to be incorporated into all plants and corrections made universally. Thus, spare part inventories could be maintained. The spare parts could be produced via batch and mass production and did not have to be produced one at a time. There also were some costs to this standardization: Errors were embodied in all plants, and in case of severe problems, all plants had to be shut down.

Communication

Learning requires effective communication of information among all those involved in a nuclear power program—vendors, architect engineers, construction companies, utilities, and regulators. When an incident occurs, for example an equipment failure, it is critical that this information be disseminated among all the parties for whom it will have consequences. All of these parties must have the chance to derive implications and to alter their practices in light of experience. In the United States, because of the complexity of the participants in the nuclear power program, this process of communication has not been smooth. In France, because of standardization, the process has worked much better.

In the United States as a whole nuclear power requires coordinating the work of 4 vendors, 12 architect-engineers, over 50 utilities and an almost equal number public utility commissions, and the NRC. Of the vendors—Westinghouse, General Electric, Babcock and Wilson, and Combustion Engineering—General Electric produces boiling water reactors (BWRs) and the other three produce pressurized water reactors (PWRs). The vendors compete against each other and lack incentive to share information. All four companies are large and diversified, with Westinghouse and General Electric producing mainly turbine generators and Babcock and Wilcox and Combustion Engineering providing steam supply systems. Together they rely on about 200 subcontractors. Westinghouse and General Electric have the longest history in the nuclear power program, having participated in the power demonstration program established by the AEC in the 1950s. The reactors ordered in the precommercial stage of development were their creations. They were awarded the first 12 turnkey (fixed-price) orders for commercial nuclear power plants and produced most subsequent reactors as well. Babcock and Wilcox and Combustion Engineering only won their first orders in 1966 after 20 reactor orders already had been placed. Their first reactors were large ones. As they never had the chance to learn from experience by scaling up their operations, not surprisingly, Babcock and Wilcox reactors have had performance difficulties. Westinghouse and General Electric reactors have not been trouble free either—Westinghouse reactors having problems with steam generator corrosion and GE reactors having difficulties with cracks in the pipe work.

Architect-engineers like Bechtel, Stone and Webster, and Sargent and Lundy design nuclear power plants and buy the components. They also construct plants, but it is not uncommon in the U.S. industry for there to be a different construction company. Some utilities (Duke Power and the Tennessee Valley Authority, or TVA) have carried out these functions themselves. In this respect they are more like the giant, government owned and operated French utility Electricite de France (EDF), which carries out all these functions. Because the architect-engineers and construction companies charge on a cost-plus basis, the delays and failures that have plagued many nuclear power projects have affected them less than the utilities. The costs to the utilities have been great, as delays and failures mean that replacement power has to be purchased and the present value of future project benefits is reduced. The architect-engineer or construction company is not always responsible for delays or failures, as regulatory disruptions, financial difficulties, and low demand for power have led many utilities to make the explicit choice to stretch out construction schedules.

Diversity

The utilities that own and operate nuclear power plants in the United States are diverse. Some are large and have strong technical leadership and engineering capability. Others are equally large but are not known for technical leadership and engineering capability. These utilities are holding companies only loosely held together, with nuclear power plants in many different parts of the country. Some of the utilities that own and operate nuclear power plants in the United States are vertically integrated, involved in nearly all stages in the production of power from mining to marketing and waste management. A few utilities have acted as their own architect-engineer and construction company. Some of the utilities that own and operate nuclear power plants in the United States have decided to take the route of unrelated diversification to protect themselves against short-term market perturbations, avoid financial losses, and achieve a position in which they can redeploy valuable staff when adversity strikes. Most of the U.S. utilities that own and operate nuclear power plants are investor owned. The exception is the TVA, which is the largest owner and operator of nuclear power plants in the United States. Public ownership should give the TVA some unique advantages, for example an ability to escape the vicissitudes of market changes, to absorb short-term setbacks, and to draw on the government's pool of skilled employees, but the TVA has had very poorly performing nuclear power plants.

Some of the utilities that own and operate nuclear power plants are located in areas of the country with rapid growth. Some utilities played a pioneering role in the nuclear power industry, ordering reactors in the precommercial stage and gaining valuable experience before constructing and operating reactors for commercial use. Other utilities put off ordering their first reactors until 1973-1974, when the large bulk of orders for reactors were made in the United States. The worst-performing nuclear power plant program in the United States in construction experience was the Washington Public Power Supply System (WPPSS). Underwritten by many local municipalities and co-ops, its aim was to construct five reactors with three different vendors and three different architect-engineers. Numerous small suppliers and subcontractors were involved. The whole project got out of managerial control, and only one unit attained final licensing and commercial operation. All the other units were canceled. WPPS ultimately defaulted on its bonds.

Self-Regulation and Regulation by the Federal Government

Only after the unfortunate TMI incident did the utilities band together for the purposes of self-regulation in a utility-wide association, the Institute for Nuclear Power Operations (INPO) (Barkenbus, 1983). INPO inspects operating plants, reviews and analyzes abnormal events, and helps individual utilities with training and emergency planning. A consortium of insurance companies that bears the risk of nuclear power operations beyond the government-guaranteed level relies on INPO reports to assess nuclear power plants. This arrangements adds some weight to INPO recommendations. Earlier industry-wide bodies, the Electric Power Research Institute (EPRI) and the Edison Electric Institute (EEI), acted as research and lobbying arms for the industry and had no supervisory functions.

Safety regulation in the United States is carried out at the national level by the NRC. Owning and operating a nuclear power plant is different from owning and operating other types of technology, because safety is such a critical consideration. Safety has to be viewed broadly, including the general public as well as operators and users. The early research in light water reactor technology was carried out by the federal government as part of the Atoms for Peace program inaugurated by President Eisenhower (see Chapter 7). The early work in scaling up the nuclear Navy submarine version of the PWR to commercial size was done in government labs with little communication or contact with the ultimate commercial users, the electric utilities. Electric utilities had little impact on the choice of technology or on the direction that technological development took.

It was not until 1974 that the AEC was split up into a regulatory body, the NRC, and a research arm that continued with its prior mission of promoting nuclear power. The two major tasks that the NRC had to deal with early in its existence were to issue construction permits to the vast number of nuclear power plants ordered at this time, and to set standards for emergency core cooling systems (ECCS), a necessary part of those reactors. Each of the newly ordered plants was somewhat different—there was no standardization in the U.S. program at that time, no real efforts to promote it, and no real understanding of the costs of the extensive customization that was taking place. With 4 vendors, more than 12 architect-engineers, and over 50 different utilities, it was not surprising that every reactor was unique and each plant required its own separate safety analysis. The requirement to deal with this diversity imposed a mighty burden on the newly created NRC.

After the TMI accident, public expectations about what the NRC should do again increased. Human factors became a central concern (see Chapter 7). The NRC imposed new requirements on control rooms, training, communications between utilities and vendors, and emergency planning. Emphasis was given to minor failures that could develop into major accidents with broad and wide-scale consequences. The NRC multiplied the number of backfits it expected that the utilities make. Each of these requirements may have made sense in isolation, but they were so numerous that they overburdened the utilities with more than they felt they could capably handle. The utilities complained that there was no system to the NRC requirements, that they were not well coordinated, and that no consideration was given to cost-effectiveness or to the potential deleterious unintended consequences. Certainly, it is true that nuclear power plant capacity factors sank after the TMI incident, although earlier they had been improving. It is also true that in the 1980s, nuclear power plant safety performance improved.

A major lesson to be learned from the utilities' experience with nuclear power is that the substitution of a capital-intensive technology that uses little fuel for a noncapital-intensive technology that consumes vast amounts of nonrenewable energy is neither an easy nor smooth process. Financial markets and institutions constitute substantial obstacles, and the adjustment capabilities of society are far from instantaneous.

The Future

The growing recognition of the importance of the greenhouse effect may make the nuclear option, along with such alternatives as photovoltaics (see Appendix 1), attractive to the utility industry. If this outcome occurs, there has to be a sustained and serious effort to commercialize "inherently safe" designs for nuclear power reactors (Golay & Todreas, 1990; Hudson, 1990; U.S. Congress, House Committee on Energy and Commerce, Subcommittee on Energy and Power, 1989a; U.S. Congress, Senate Committee on Energy and Natural Resources, Subcommittee on Energy Research and Development, 1988). For instance, the Integral Fast Reactor (IFR) is an advanced nuclear reactor concept that has become a focus of DOE's reactor research and development program. The purpose of the IFR program is to provide an advanced reactor technology to overcome the problems of today's reactors. The IFR reactor is cooled by liquid sodium at low pressure and fueled by a new metal alloy fuel. The fuel is reprocessed with a new technology called pyroprocessing and refabricated into new metal fuel rods for recycling to the reactor.

Improved assurance of reactor safety is a main objective of the IFR. Compared to existing reactors, safety of the IFR relies more on inherently passive characteristics of the system and less on the proper functioning of complex engineered systems and operators taking correct action. In tests of IFR, conditions were created that would be expected to lead to severe meltdown in most types of reactors. The IFR prototype simply shut itself down without operator intervention and without damage of any kind. Improved nuclear waste management is another goal of the IFR. The pyroprocess is supposed to keep all the very long-lived carcinogenic materials together with the fuel for recycling back to the reactor. The period that these nuclear wastes would be harmful would decline to hundreds from millions of years.

Atmospheric warming (see Appendix 2) may mean that alternative nuclear reactor designs like the IFR will become increasingly important. If nuclear power is to substitute for conventional sources of power generation, such as coal and oil, that produce vast amounts of carbon dioxide, then new reactors based on different designs will be needed (Sillen, 1988).

9

Conclusion

Energy is essential for the world economy. A key factor in the production process, it is among the most critical of the natural resources needed to make the goods and services upon which people depend. Energy is also a major source of pollution and waste. Its extraction, transportation, transformation, and use cause major environmental and safety problems. Even without the complications of international politics, the problems of energy production and use, simply because of the environmental and safety issues, would be great. But the complications of international politics raise energy issues to nearly the top of the policy agenda in the emerging post-cold war era.

For world prosperity, it is essential that there be stability in world energy markets. If unimpeded by political forces—whether international or domestic—markets would reflect increasing energy scarcity in higher prices. Higher prices would then cause adjustments in the behavior of individuals, corporations, and nations, inducing conservation and stimulating the search for new sources of supply. High prices would also provide incentives for technological innovations to lower extraction costs and lead to new, more efficient energy use. The market system, if unimpeded by politics, is an effective way to bring about all these adjustments. This is not to say that the market is without imperfections. The true social costs of energy use, which include damage to the environment and concerns for national security, have to be reflected in energy prices. The government role is to tax energy to reflect its true social costs—a task that the U.S. government has shrunk from doing, although governments in other nations of the world have been more willing to accept this responsibility.

The Energy Policy System

The key elements in the energy policy system which have been the focus of this book are portrayed in Figure 9.1. Labor, natural resources, and capital combine to make the goods and services people use. This process produces numerous by-products and wastes that society has to handle. The core use of energy in the production system is affected by and in turn affects many other systems, as depicted in the figure.

If everything else were equal, the main influence on the use of energy would be the market. Prices would determine the types of energy used, where, and in what quantities. But everything else is not equal. Energy markets do not operate as freely as economic doctrine holds. With a high proportion of world energy reserves controlled by unstable Persian Gulf countries at times unfriendly to the West, the movement of world energy resources often has been blocked for purely political reasons. The flow of world energy resources has not without impediment always gone to the highest bidder. The OPEC nations came together with the express intention of preventing energy from moving freely from producer to consumer in response to market forces.

As economic doctrine predicts, cartels are able to achieve short-term successes, because people do not instantaneously adjust to rapid and unanticipated increases in energy prices. Energy-inefficient capital equipment becomes outmoded, but it is not replaced immediately. People's old habits of consumption resist change. It takes time for society to adjust to higher energy prices, and the adjustment process can be painful.

OPEC was able to enjoy short-term successes, but in the long run its very successes undermined its capabilities. Higher-priced energy, forced on the world by the OPEC-induced supply interruptions of 1973 and 1979, stimulated conservation and led to the search for new energy supplies. The supply interruptions also damaged the world economy to the point where energy demand declined and the OPEC nations themselves suffered. With less energy demand in the world, the power of the OPEC nations diminished.

Partially because of OPEC's unraveling (and partially because of the megalomania of the Iraqi leader Saddam Hussein), Iraq took upon itself

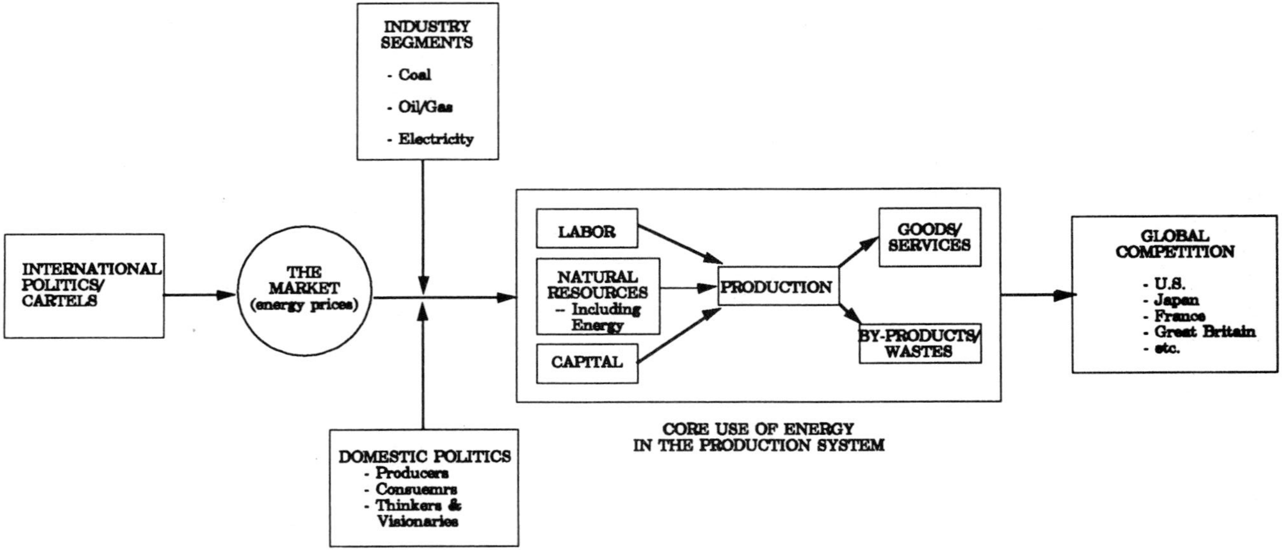

Figure 9.1. The Energy Policy System

the ambition to be the dominant force among the OPEC countries. Its economy had been ravished because of its senseless war with Iran, and it was desperate to gain revenue from higher oil prices; but with OPEC's reduced power, this opportunity was not available. For Iraq, oil was not simply a means for providing for jobs and development in an area that had suffered from nearly 10 years of unrelenting war. It was a means for acquiring Western technology and weapons. Thus, political instability among the nations that control most of the world's petroleum led to the tragic war of the United States and its allies against Iraq.

Inability to Reduce Dependence

Energy, then, is a commodity whose production and use are not simply determined by market forces. Nonmarket forces—specifically international political tensions—have caused major supply interruptions that have done irreparable damage to the world economy. The ability of cartels to threaten world prosperity partially derives from the inability of developed countries to sufficiently reduce their dependence on petroleum from unstable regions of the globe. Although substantial progress was made following past energy hikes, it was not great enough to reduce the vulnerabilities. Some of the responsibility lies with U.S. politicians. The United States consumes more energy per capita than any nation in the world, but U.S. politicians were unwilling to use the price system to reflect the true social cost of energy production and to thereby stimulate conservation, the search for new supplies, and other types of technological innovation.

Such a tax scheme might be acceptable if it were implemented in a gradual, phased manner. Gradual, phased, and *planned* energy price hikes imposed by a society *on itself* are to be preferred to sudden price hikes imposed externally by enemies of that society. The unplanned and unanticipated price hikes do great economic damage that the planned and anticipated price hikes would not cause. The adjustment process to planned and anticipated price rises is certain to be smoother and more effective than the adjustment process to unplanned, unanticipated price rises imposed from without.

Running Out of Energy?

From an economic point of view, the world does *not* run the risk of running out of energy—the energy problem does not consist of the depletion of a nonrenewable resource. When a resource becomes scarce, prices simply go up and society adjusts. The energy problem is rather one of unexpected disruptions of energy supplies by foreign governments intent on achieving political objectives. The unpreparedness of consuming nations for these interruptions makes them and their societies vulnerable. The mistaken policies they adopt in response to the unexpected price rises adds to their vulnerability. In the United States the character of these policies is familiar. The government tries to protect consumer groups from the consequences of price increases rather than letting them experience the full impact and adjust accordingly.

The U.S. government was manipulated by a variety of strong interests wishing to exploit the political process to serve their ideological or narrow economic interests. Some viewed energy issues as part of a broader critique of U.S. society and used the issues to promote a vision of society that was smaller, less bureaucratic, less focused on the military, and less enamored with "hard" energy technologies such as nuclear power. They called on the government to reverse past subsidy policies and focus federal efforts on solar power and conservation. Other groups continued to fight for favorable government treatment for the established energy industries such as petroleum, coal, and nuclear power. In many instances the representatives of the established energy industries lost crucial political battles to the new breed of energy planners and visionaries. The established industries faced a hostile political and economic climate where they were not always politically or economically dominant. But they were able to maintain some portion of the subsidies and protected status that they formerly enjoyed.

The old order eroded piecemeal and in its place a new group of energy policies emerged. The new energy policies, like the old, had no overall plan associated with them. They were partial in character and lacked broad justification and coherence. The landscape for the energy industries in the United States continued to be extraordinarily complex with pure market forces remarkably absent and strange combinations of subsidies, protection, and partially free markets operating in different energy arenas.

International Dimensions

As in almost all policy areas today, energy issues cannot be understood in their purely domestic context. Thus I have emphasized in this book the important international dimensions of energy issues, starting with OPEC and moving to the responses of the major consuming nations. OPEC's very existence as a cartel is an affront to the principles of a free economy that hold that commodities should not be artificially withheld from the market but should be allowed to compete on a free and equal basis. The laws of economics, of supply and demand, have in the end caught up with OPEC, as they do with almost all cartels, but in between OPEC's actions hurt the world economy.

The international dimensions of world energy problems also must be understood in the capabilities of different countries to respond to sudden energy price spikes. Different countries have adopted different kinds of responses, and with these different responses have come different results. Japan has tried to increase its international competitiveness to pay for higher-priced petroleum products. Rather than shielding its economy from the higher petroleum prices, it added energy taxes and created programs that forced industries to conserve. It also searched for alternative energy sources and found them in LNG and nuclear energy. Likewise the French were among the world's most successful nations in reducing their dependence on petroleum by developing an alternative energy industry on a vast scale—nuclear power—and by stressing conservation. Great Britain was fortunate in discovering new energy supplies in the North Sea that made it independent of foreign oil, but paradoxically this new-found capability to be independent of foreign oil did not greatly help the British economy. Rather it diverted capital from more productive sectors to the highly inefficient nationalized energy sector. Similarly the Soviet Union, also rich in petroleum, was not able to take advantage of the situation to create sustained economic gain.

The examples of these countries should warn energy policymakers that achieving the goal of energy independence in and of itself does not guarantee a nation economic vitality. Economic vitality is tied to technological virtuosity and a world market orientation, both of which were achieved to a greater extent by Japan and France than by Great Britain or the Soviet Union.

Alternative Energy Industries

The role of the U.S. government in trying to develop alternative energy industries has been the topic of the last portion of this book. The record here is very mixed. Certainly in the case of shale oil the U.S. government escaped making a premature commitment to an expensive and environmentally harmful alternative to foreign petroleum, but the fact that it came so close to carrying out this campaign should give pause. Why did it come so close to making a wrong-headed commitment, and should it have a correct commitment to make, will it have the political will to carry through with it? Is government support for the development of any alternative energy industry possible in the United States, given the contentious and fractious nature of U.S. politics?

The history of nuclear power is longer and the commitment of the U.S. government to this form of energy is deeper, but it shares many of the features displayed in the more condensed history of synfuels. Initial enthusiasm and unlimited support was followed by a period of reconsideration and dissipated enthusiasm as political opposition grew and the real problems with this technology became apparent. The development of nuclear power was initially framed almost exclusively in technical terms and human and safety issues were overlooked. It took the tragic TMI accident to bring these concerns to the forefront, but by this time acceptance of nuclear power had dissipated.

A remaining question of great importance is how the electric utilities in the United States will meet future demands for power. Electricity demand continued to grow, although demand for other forms of power leveled off and declined after 1973. Electricity demand growth was not as great as it had been before 1973, but it remained strong. Electricity was arguably the most advanced form of power, as it offered many advantages over other energy types, but where and how future sources of electricity would be generated and how the electric utility industry in the United States would be managed were open questions. A new type of nuclear reactor design with more forgiving safety features seemed to be necessary, but could the U.S. government—or for that matter any government in the world—sustain a program to develop a new nuclear technology given the world's attitudes toward this technology?

Politics and Markets

With questions of politics and markets the analysis in this book comes to a final and perhaps most important point. Economic doctrine maintains that the price system is the most effective means for achieving transitions from one technological domain to another. The government has a long-term role to play, but better definition of this role is needed. The issue is particularly pressing in a society like that of the United States where the government is open to so many diverse interests. Besides taxing energy appropriately, the government should support long-term research and development, but in which areas? How to choose how much support should be given and for how long are difficult questions to resolve in a democracy with so much freedom of access and so much interest group power.

Clearly, the government's role should not be to shield people from the consequences of higher energy prices. Energy prices should be allowed to rise to the level of their true social cost, which includes the national security and environmental costs of energy production, and the government should stick to this principle so that the private sector has a sense of a steady energy policy around which it can plan. Then, in the face of calculations of the returns from long-run capital-intensive energy investments, the private sector can make better choices about which options to pursue. Out of this process a mix of energy types and conservation policies is likely to evolve to supply the energy needs of the future.

Politically Inspired Shortages

To conclude, the major, unanticipated price hikes of the last 20 years, which have been so damaging to the world economy, have been politically motivated. They are not the result of scarcity, that is, the world running out of or depleting an essential resource. They are also not the result of the extensive environmental damage caused by the use of energy, which is a very real and important problem, but one that has not been adequately addressed by world governments. Rather the supply interruptions have come about for political reasons that go far beyond the realm of economics.

The desire on the part of the OPEC nations to subvert free markets is not a matter of the pursuit of self-interest by other means. Rather, the supply interruptions have their roots in much broader political and historical yearnings that are the vestiges of perceptions of Western arrogance and domination and Middle Eastern technological inferiority. It is the intertwining of economics and politics that makes the energy policy system so complicated and so dangerous.

APPENDIX 1

Photovoltaics

A photovoltaic (PV) cell produces electricity directly from sunlight (Buchholz, Marcus, & Post, 1992). When the sunlight strikes the surface of the semiconductor material of which the cell is made, it energizes some of the semiconductor's electrons enough to break them loose. The loose electrons are channeled through a metallic grid on the cell's surface to junctions where they are combined with electrons from other cells to form an electric current. Electrons of different semiconductor materials are broken loose by different wavelengths of light, and some wavelengths of sunlight reach the earth's surface with more intensity than others. Consequently, much of the effort of PV research has been to find semiconductor materials that are energized by the light wavelengths that are most intense and have the potential to provide the most energy.

Photovoltaics are not the only way of utilizing the sun's energy. In fact, PVs are not even the major producer of electricity from sunlight. That distinction belongs to solar thermal technologies. Solar thermal systems work by using the heating rays of the sun to warm air, water, or oil for space heating or thermal power generation. Luz International of Los Angeles is the world's largest producer of solar thermal electric plants. The company's seven plants in California's Mojave Desert produce 90% of all solar-generated power in the world. Company officials estimate that solar thermal plants occupying just 1% of the Mojave could supply all of Southern California Edison's peak power requirements. Solar thermal facilities, which on sunny days can achieve conversion efficiencies twice that of some PVs, generate power at a cost equal to late-generation nuclear plants, and the cost is dropping.

Single-crystal silicon cells were the first type of PVs widely used, powering satellite radios as early as 1958. These cells are energized by some of the most intense sunlight wavelengths and have achieved conversion efficiencies (percentage of light energy converted to electricity) over 20%. Other, non-silicon, single-crystal cells have achieved efficiencies over 27%. Although efficient, these single-crystal cells are also expensive to produce and the crystals are difficult to grow. Much of the crystal is wasted when it is sawed into pieces for individual PV cells. Because the cost is so much, use has been limited mainly to applications where electricity is necessary and there are no other alternatives, such as in the space program.

To reduce production costs, researchers began to search for ways to fabricate silicon into cells that did not require the expensive and wasteful single-crystal techniques. One result of their efforts are *polycrystalline silicon cells,* which sacrifice some efficiency in return for cheaper manufacturing methods. The most efficient polycrystalline cells to date achieve better than 15% efficiencies. Together, single-crystal and polycrystalline cells account for two thirds of those sold. Perhaps the most promising PV technologies are the "thin-film" techniques, in which cells as large as 4 square feet—crystalline cells are in the neighborhood of 1/4 inch in diameter—are produced by depositing a film of PV material less than one hundredth the thickness of a crystalline cell on a suitable base, or substrate. These cells are only about half as efficient as single-crystal cells, but because they can be produced for about one fourth the cost or less, they offer the greatest potential for large-scale use. Thin-film silicon cells (called *amorphous silicon*) accounted for 37% of the world market for PVs in 1987. One drawback to amorphous silicon cells, however, is that they typically lose about one sixth of their power output in the first few months of use. There are other thin-film materials that do not suffer from this light-induced degradation. Two of the most promising are copper indium diselenide (CIS) and cadmium telluride (CdTe).

The world leader in CIS technology was ARCO Solar, Inc. The company developed a 4-square-foot CIS cell with a 9% conversion efficiency, demonstrating that large-scale applications of thin-film technology are feasible. A Texas company, Photon Energy, Inc., developed an inexpensive, simple process for applying CdTe to panels as large as ARCO's, achieving 7% efficiency. The company managed better than 12% efficiencies in the laboratory and expects to do even better in the near future.

Besides improving conversion efficiencies by developing new PV compounds, researchers have broken efficiency records by "stacking" cells. *Mechanically stacked multijunction* (MSMJ) cells are actually two cells pasted together. The top cell extracts the energy from one part of the light spectrum, and the lower cell uses the energy from a different part. A MSMJ cell composed of a single-crystal gallium arsenide cell and a single-crystal silicon cell has achieved a better than 30% efficiency, and researchers believe that a three-layer cell with 38% efficiency is possible. Efficiency improvements via stacking of more economical thin-film cells are also being investigated.

The continuing improvements in conversion efficiencies are especially remarkable considering that as recently as 1982, theoretical physicists believed that the maximum achievable efficiency of a solar cell was 22%. The highest efficiency achieved at that point was 16%. Now theoreticians estimate that 38%-40% is the limit, although the physics of thin-film technology is not completely understood (U.S. Congress, Senate Committee on Energy and Natural Resources, Subcommittee on Energy Research and Development, 1987a).

APPENDIX 2

Global Warming

Human activities of the past 100 years appear to be altering the composition of the atmosphere, causing a global warming trend (Moore, 1988). Many scientists already are convinced that global warming has started and that it will worsen through the next century. In the past century, they estimate that the globe warmed between 0.5°C and 2°C. Warming occurs by means of the greenhouse effect, that is, the trapping of infrared energy, or heat, in the stratosphere. Trapping of such heat is caused by carbon dioxide and other greenhouse gases chemically interacting with additional atmospheric gases. The greenhouse gases, including carbon dioxide, are transparent to sunlight, thus letting the energy penetrate the earth. Absorbing most of the sunlight, the earth converts the light energy into heat. Any light that is not absorbed is reflected back into space by means of clouds, ice, and snow. As the heat rises from the earth, it strikes the carbon dioxide and other greenhouse gases. Some of the heat is reflected back again to the earth, causing the warming effect in the same way that a greenhouse works, with panes of glass that allow higher energy light waves to enter easily, but do not allow the heat of lower energy to escape.

In discussing the greenhouse effect, major emphasis is placed on carbon dioxide because it makes up about 50% of the problem. In 1990, carbon dioxide was measured in the atmosphere to be approximately 344 parts per million (ppm). This amount was large considering that only 100 years ago the carbon dioxide concentration was only 293 ppm. Thus, an increase of about 15% had occurred in the last 100 years. The major cause of the increased volume of carbon dioxide is the burning of fossil fuels like oil, coal, and gasoline. Scientists tend to be pessimistic about the likely curtailment in the use of fossil fuel, thus estimating an increase in carbon dioxide emissions of 0.5% to 2% per year for the next several decades.

The other gases making up the remaining 50% of the greenhouse effect are methane, chlorofluorocarbons (CFCs), nitrous oxides, and ozone. Currently, the atmosphere contains 100% more methane than it did during glacier periods. This increase is caused by the harvesting of rice paddies, the use of landfills, and the flaring of natural gas wells. Methane contributes about 20% of the greenhouse effect. CFCs emitted from the earth are found in the atmosphere at one part per billion. They constitute about 15% of the total greenhouse gases. Nitrous oxides, found in the atmosphere in minute traces, originate from the use of fertilizers, the natural process of the emittance of soil microbes, and the burning of fossil fuels. Nitrous oxides emissions account for about 10% of the greenhouse effect. The last major gas that contributes to the greenhouse effect is ozone. Even though the ozone layer provides ultraviolet protection at high levels in the atmosphere, at lower levels, where it is more commonly known as smog, this gas is dangerous. Ozone contributes about 5% of the greenhouse effect.

Three known natural processes may counteract the greenhouse effect. These are the absorption of the carbon dioxide by the oceans, absorption by tropical rain forests and other vegetation, and reflection of sunlight back into space by the clouds. The oceans are considered to be the major sink for carbon dioxide gas, as carbon dioxide gas is readily dissolved into seawater; aquatic plants absorb this carbon and when these plants die they take the carbon out of the natural life cycle. It is not known how much carbon dioxide is absorbed by the oceans. Because of the oceans' vastness, scientists find it difficult to estimate the exact amounts of carbon dioxide plants absorb and how much oxygen they produce through photosynthesis. The rate of absorption by plants is estimated to be 500 billion tons of carbon dioxide annually worldwide, but this estimate is very uncertain. Because of rapid deforestation it could be decreasing rapidly.

Clouds counteract heat retention not by absorbing carbon dioxide, but by reflecting sunlight back into outer space. If the infrared light from the sun does not reach the earth, heat cannot be created. If the heat on the earth's surface does not go up, the greenhouse effect cannot occur. When infrared light does reach the earth, clouds may then reflect the heat back toward the earth, thus warming it. Major uncertainty exists about the role of clouds in counteracting the greenhouse effect. Ultimately this matter is extremely complicated, because it depends on subtle distinctions of cloud thickness.

There are many impacts that the greenhouse effect can have on the world (Cahan & Bremner, 1989). Some of the major consequences that have been predicted are listed below. These predictions assume that the levels of carbon dioxide and the other greenhouse gases will be emitted at the same rate as present:

- In Greenland and the Arctic, some of the permafrost and ice will melt, causing the oceans to rise and threatening flooding along coastal areas.
- The midwestern United States will be hit hard by drought conditions due to the warmer weather evaporating more water, causing drier soils.

- With the increased evaporation of water, rivers will decrease in level, thus causing a shortage in water supplies, lower generation of power, and a disruption in agricultural irrigation.
- The former republics of the Soviet Union will gain approximately 40 more days in their growing season, which could make them a net exporter of grain to the rest of the world.
- The increased temperatures will cause a wider area of rain forest growth, moving the African rain forests north and bringing rain to Chad, Sudan, and Ethiopia, breaking their prolonged dry spell.
- An increase in snow and frozen rain in Antarctica will create a thicker ice level that will help counteract some of the greenhouse effect by reflecting more sunlight and counteracting the sea level rise.

Canada and the United States have the highest emissions levels of greenhouse gases per capita among the developed Western democracies. The highest level of greenhouse gas emissions per capita in the world, however, is found in East Germany. Brazil and the Ivory Coast have the highest levels of emissions per capita among developing countries, and per unit of GNP, Brazil's and India's emissions of greenhouse gases surpass the levels found in the United States.

A first approach to limiting carbon dioxide buildup would be making energy supply and use more efficient (U.S. Congress, Senate Committee on Energy and Natural Resources, 1987b, 1989). Examples of available technology for conservation are increasingly efficient light bulbs in commercial buildings, better insulated buildings, and the manufacture of more fuel-efficient vehicles. Prototype vehicles have obtained up to 70 mpg. U.S. fuel standards for new vehicles have been set at 27 mpg. As the vehicle stock turns over, the overall fleet average is increased. A fleet average of 40 mpg with no increase in miles driven would cut U.S. auto-related carbon emissions in half.

Another option to reduce the use of fossil fuels is to use different sources of energy. Alternatives such as nuclear power, hydropower, and natural gas produce far less carbon dioxide. The Bush administration has proposed that methanol be given serious consideration as an alternative motor vehicle fuel. Methanol made from biomass (primarily wood, organic wastes, or agricultural produce) would not contribute to greenhouse emissions as long as the biomass feedstock was replaced. Hydrogen, however, appears to be the best long-term alternative means for motor vehicle propulsion. A hydrogen-based fuel would emit only water vapor and nitrous oxides, the latter at significantly lower levels than produced by fossil fuels. Estimates of hydrogen's costs place it at \$2-\$4 per gallon equivalent shortly after the year 2000, which would make it competitive with gasoline if gas taxes were increased to reflect gasoline's true social cost. A big problem is fuel tank storage. Fuel efficiency gains are needed so that smaller tanks can be used without sacrificing the range of hydrogen cars.

Another problem with the fuel tank is safety. A final problem with hydrogen is how to safely and efficiently manufacture it.

Another method to reduce carbon dioxide buildup is to end the deforestation of the world's rain forests. The burning of the rain forests emits an estimated 1 billion tons of carbon dioxide a year, and at the same time the earth loses one of its major sinks to absorb carbon dioxide. Encouraging the reforestation of areas of the globe that have been denuded of their natural tree cover is a gesture of important symbolic significance, but it cannot make an important dent in carbon dioxide buildup.

A final method to reduce carbon dioxide buildup is to concentrate future energy research and development on noncarbon-based fuels. Photovoltaics are an excellent example. If they became commercially feasible on a large scale, they could make an important dent in the greenhouse problem.

References

Ahearne, J. F. (1983). Prospects for the U.S. nuclear reactor industry. *Annual Review of Energy, 8,* 355-384.

Ahrari, M. E. (1986). *OPEC: The falling giant.* Lexington, KY: University Press of Kentucky.

Alm, A. L., & Weiner, R. J. (Eds.). (1984). *Oil shock: Policy response and implementation.* Cambridge, MA: Ballinger.

Anderson, D. (1981). *Regulatory politics and electric utilities.* Cambridge, MA: Auburn House.

Anderson, G. H., Bryan, M. F., & Pike, C. J. (1990, November 1). Oil, the economy, and monetary policy. *Economic Commentary.* Federal Reserve Bank of Cleveland.

Aperjis, D. G. (1984). Oil export policy and economic development in OPEC. *Annual Review of Energy, 9,* 179-198.

Barkenbus, J. N. (1983). Is self-regulation possible? *Journal of Policy Analysis and Management, 4,* 576-588.

Bending, R., Cattell, R., & Eden, R. (1987). Energy and structural change in the United Kingdom and western Europe. *Annual Review of Energy, 12,* 185-222.

Berndt, E. R., & Wood, D. O. (1987). Energy price shocks and productivity growth: A survey. In R. L. Gordon, H. D. Jacoby, & M. B. Zimmerman (Eds.), *Energy* (pp. 305-343). Cambridge, MA: MIT Press.

Biddle, F. M. (1990, August 12). Playing the oil reserve ace. *Boston Globe,* p. A1.

Bohi, D. R. (1989). *Energy price shocks and macroeconomic performance.* Washington, DC: Resources for the Future.

Broad, W. J. (1990, October 9). Next bold step toward fusion proposed. *New York Times,* p. B5.

Brooks, G., & Horwitz, T. (1990, August 13). Gulf crisis underscores historical divisions in the Arab "family." *Wall Street Journal,* p. A1.

Brown, W. M. (1981, November 30). Can OPEC survive the glut? *Fortune,* pp. 89-96.

Buchholz, R., Marcus A., & Post, J. (1992). *Managing environmental issues: A case book.* Englewood Cliffs, NJ: Prentice-Hall.

Cahan, V., & Bremner, B. (1989, February 13). When the rivers go dry and the ice caps melt . . . . *Business Week,* pp. 95-98.

Campbell, J. (1988). *Collapse of an industry.* Ithaca, NY: Cornell University Press.

Carter, S. (1986). The changing structure of energy industries in the United Kingdom. *Annual Review of Energy, 11,* 451-469.

Chandler, A., & Brauchli, M. W. (1990, September 10). How Japan became so energy-efficient: It leaned on industry. *Wall Street Journal,* p. A1.

Corrigan, R. (1979, November 10). The ill-advised rush to synfuels. *National Journal,* p. 1284.

Corrigan, R. (1983, March 14). Synfuels subsidies—Reports of their death are greatly exaggerated. *National Journal,* p. 430.

Daly, H. (1979). Entropy, growth, and the political economy of scarcity. In V. K. Smith (Ed.), *Scarcity and growth reconsidered* (pp. 67-95). Baltimore, MD: Johns Hopkins University Press.

Darmstadter, J, Landsberg, J. H., Morton, H. C., & Coda, M. J. (1983). *Energy, today and tomorrow: Living with uncertainty.* Englewood Cliffs, NJ: Prentice-Hall.

Del Sesto, S. L. (1982). The rise and fall of nuclear power in the United States and the limits of regulation. *Technology In Society, 4,* 295-314.

Emshwiller, J. R. (1990, October 30). Energy-efficiency guru sees fertile field for start-ups. *Wall Street Journal,* p. B2.

Energy Information Administration. (1987). *Annual energy outlook: 1987.* Washington, DC: Author.

Energy Information Administration. (1989, October). *Short-term energy outlook: Quarterly projections.* Washington, DC: Author.

Energy taxes for America. (1990, July 21). *Economist,* p. 11.

Erol, U., & Yu, E. (1988). On the causal relationship between energy and income for industrialized countries. *Journal of Energy and Development, 13*(1), 113-139.

Fenn, S. (1983). *America's electric utilities under siege and in transition.* Washington, DC: Investor Responsibility Research Center.

Ford, D. (1982). *Cult of the atom: The secret papers of the Atomic Energy Commission.* New York: Simon & Schuster.

Friedman, M., & Friedman, R. (1980). *Free to Choose.* New York: Avon.

Gately, D. (1986a). Lessons from the 1986 oil price collapse. In W. C. Brainard & G. L. Perry (Eds.), *Economic activity 2* (pp. 237-287). Washington, DC: Brookings Institution.

Gately, D. (1986b). The prospects for oil prices revisited. *Annual Review of Energy, 11,* 513-588.

Geller, H. (1987). The role of federal research and development in advancing energy efficiency: A $50 billion contribution to the U.S. economy. *Annual Review of Energy, 12,* 357-395.

Giraud, A. (1983). Energy in France. *Annual Review of Energy, 8,* 165-191.

Golay, M. W., & Todreas, N. E. (1990, April). Advanced light-water reactors. *Scientific American,* pp. 82-89.

Greenhouse, S. (1990, August 31). Oil shortage is seen by year-end. *New York Times,* p. C3.

Gumbel, P., & Tanner, J. (1990, August 22). Soviet oil industry, mismanaged for years, can't fill Iraq gap. *Wall Street Journal,* p. A1.

Gutfeld, R. (1990, September 26). Senate supporters of fuel economy bill lose vote, dooming measure this year. *Wall Street Journal,* p. A2.

Hershey, R. D., Jr. (1980, September 21). Energy: Blessing or boondoggle? *New York Times,* p. 1B.

Hershey, R. D., Jr. (1983, May 12). Synthetic fuels: Program lags. *New York Times,* p. 430.

Hewett, E. A. (1984). *Energy, economics, and foreign policy in the Soviet Union.* Washington, DC: Brookings Institution.

How big an oil shock? (1990, August 11). *Economist,* pp. 12-13.

Hudson, R. L. (1990, May 22). Soviets pushing for ultrasafe reactors. *Wall Street Journal,* p. A19.

Huntington, H. G. (1985). Oil prices and inflation. *Annual Review of Energy, 10,* 317-339.

Ibrahim, Y. M. (1982, March 8). Latest oil uncertainty concerns drop in price rather than big rise. *Wall Street Journal,* p. 1.

Iraqi invasion raises oil prices, threatens U.S., other economies. (1990, August 3). *Wall Street Journal,* p. A1.

Jestin-Fleury, N. (1988). Energy conservation in France. *Annual Review of Energy, 13,* 159-183.

Jewell, J. E., Selkowitz, S., & Verderber, R. (1980, January). Solid-state ballasts prove to be energy savers. *Lighting Design & Application,* pp. 36-42.

Jochem, E., & Morovic, T. (1988). Energy use patterns in common market countries since 1979. *Annual Review of Energy, 13,* 131-157.

Johnson, H. D. (1981). Financing synthetic fuel projects: An overview. *University of Pittsburgh Law Review, 43,* 103.

Joskow, D. (1988). The evolution of competition in the electric power industry. *Annual Review of Energy, 13,* 215-238.

Kanovsky, E. (1990, November 30). The coming oil glut. *Wall Street Journal,* p. A14.

Kaufman, A. (1984). Public policy and synthetic fuels: Challenges to business solidarity. In L. Preston (Ed.), *Research in corporate social performance and policy.* Vol. 6. Greenwich, CT: JAI.

Kemeny, J. G. (Chairman). (1979). *The need for a change: The legacy of TMI.* (Report of the President's Commission on the Accident at Three Mile Island). Washington, DC.

Kilburn, P. T. (1984, June 9). Split over U.S. budget deficits ruffles the overall harmony at London meeting. *New York Times,* p. A6.

Kim, Young-Pyoung. (1982). *Justifications of policy error correction: A case study of error correction in the Three Mile Island nuclear power plant accident.* Doctoral Dissertation, Indiana University.

Krauss, A. (1990, September 13). Bush energy plan greeted coolly; reversing output decline unlikely. *Investor's Daily,* p. A20.

Levine, M. (1985). A decade of United States energy policy. *Annual Review of Energy, 10,* 557-587.

Lonnroth, M. (1983). The European transition from oil. *Annual Review of Energy, 8,* 1-25.

Lovins, A. B. (1977). *Soft energy paths: Toward a durable peace.* New York: Friends of the Earth International.

Lowinger, D., Wihlborg, S., & Willman, T. (1986). An empirical analysis of OPEC and non-OPEC behavior. *Journal of Energy and Development, 11*(2), 119-141.

MacAvoy, P. W. (1983). *Energy policy.* New York: Norton.

Marcus, A. (1984) *The adversary economy.* Westport, CT: Greenwood.

Marcus, A., & Kaufman A. (1986). Why it is difficult to implement industrial policies: Lessons from the synfuels experience. *California Management Review, 28,* 98-115.

McCracken, P. W. (1990, October 20). The need for energy taxes. *Wall Street Journal,* p. A20.

McKie, J. (1984). Federal energy regulation. *Annual Review of Energy, 9,* 321-349.

Mead, W. (1986). The OPEC cartel thesis reexamined: Price constraints from oil substitutes. *Journal of Energy and Development, 11*(2), 213-242.

Medina, D. D. (1990, September 28). Airlines resort to penny-pinching ploys to bring their fuel bills back to earth. *Wall Street Journal,* p. B1.

Mirowski, P. (1988). Energy and energetics in economic theory: A review essay. *Journal of Economic Issues, 3,* 811-830.

Moore, A. H. (1988, July 4). A warming world. *Fortune,* pp. 102-107.

Mossavar-Rahmani, B. (1988). Japan's oil sector outlook. *Annual Review of Energy, 13,* 185-213.

Murray, A., & Wessel, D. (1990, August 6). Iraqi invasion boosts chances of recession in the U.S. this year. *Wall Street Journal,* p. A1.

Navarro, P. (1985). *The dimming of America.* Cambridge, MA: Ballinger.

Nivola, P. S. (1986). *The politics of energy conservation.* Washington, DC: Brookings Institution.

Nulty, P. (1980, September 8). The tortuous road to synfuels. *Fortune,* pp. 58-64.

Oil's economic threat is less than in '70s. (1990, August 20). *Wall Street Journal,* p. A1.

Okrent, D. (1982). *Nuclear regulatory safety.* Madison, WI: University of Wisconsin Press.

Pindyck, R. S. (Ed.). (1979). *Advances in the economics of energy and resources.* Greenwich, CT: JAI.

Pindyck, R., & Rotemberg, J. (1984). Energy shocks and the marcroeconomy. In A. L. Alm & R. J. Weiner (Eds.), *Oil Shock: Policy response and implementation* (pp. 97-121). Cambridge, MA; Ballinger.

Plattner, A. (1983, May 24). Energy issues shoved onto back burner. *Congressional Quarterly,* p. 1650.

Ramstetter, E. (1986). Interaction between Japanese policy priorities: Energy and trade in the 1980s. *Journal of Energy and Development, 11*(2), 285-301.

Razavi, H. (1989). *The new era of petroleum trading: Spot oil, spot-related contracts, and futures markets.* Washington, DC: World Bank.

Rising oil-import bill will slow trade gains. (1990, March 5). *Wall Street Journal,* p. A1.

Rogovin, M. (Director, Nuclear Regulatory Commission Special Inquiry Group). (1980). *Three Mile Island: A Report to the commissioners and to the public.* Vols. 1 & 2, Parts 1-3. (NUREG/CR 1250). Washington, DC: U.S. Nuclear Regulatory Commission.

Rolph, E. S. (1979). *Nuclear power and the public safety.* Lexington, MA: D.C. Heath.

Rosenbaum, W. A. (1987). *Energy, politics, and public policy.* Washington, DC: Congressional Quarterly Press.

Russo, M. (1989). *Generating strategy: A dynamic analysis of regulation and diversification in the electric utility industry.* Unpublished doctoral dissertation, University of California, Berkeley, Haas School of Management, 90-116.

Sakisaka, M. (1985). Japan's energy supply/demand structure and its trade relationship with the United States and the Middle East. *Journal of Energy and Development, 10*(1), 1-11.

Samii, M.V. (1985). The organization of the petroleum exporting countries and the oil market: Different views. *Journal of Energy and Development, 10,* 159-173.
Samuels, R. J. (1987). *The business of the Japanese state.* Ithaca, NY: Cornell University Press.
Schon, D. A. (1971). *Beyond the stable state.* New York: Norton.
Schurr, S. H. (Ed.). (1979). *Energy in America's future: The choices before us.* Baltimore, MD: Johns Hopkins University Press.
Schurr, S. H. (1987). Energy use, technological change, and productive efficiency. *Annual Review of Energy, 9,* 409-425.
Schwartz, P. (1987). What happened to the energy crisis? The dilemma of an energy decision maker in a dynamic world. *Annual Review of Energy, 12,* 397-414.
Shaaf, M. (1985). Strong dollar, low inflation, and OPEC'S terms of trade. *Journal of Energy and Development, 10*(1), 121-128.
Sillen, J. (1988, September 21). Nuclear medicine for energy ills. *Wall Street Journal,* p. 24.
Sills, D. L., Wolf, C. P., & Shelanski, V. B. (Eds.). (1982). *Accident at Three Mile Island: The human dimensions.* Boulder, CO: Westview.
Simon, J. L. (1981). *The ultimate resource.* Princeton, NJ: Princeton University Press.
Smith, V. K. (Ed.). (1979). *Scarcity and growth reconsidered.* Baltimore, MD: Johns Hopkins University Press.
Smith, V. K., & Krutilla, J. (1979). The economics of natural resource scarcity: An interpretive introduction. In V. K. Smith (Ed.), *Scarcity and growth reconsidered* (pp. 1-36). Baltimore, MD: Johns Hopkins University Press.
Solo, R. A. (1987). Developing an energy alternative. In R. L. Ender & J. C. Kim (Eds.), *Energy resources development: Politics and policies.* New York: Quorum.
Solomon, C. (1990, August 6). Sudden impact: Prices at U.S. gas pumps soar. *Wall Street Journal,* p. B1.
Solomon, C., & Gutfeld, R. (1990). Petroleum reserve has lots of oil, but using it could be a challenge. *Wall Street Journal,* p. A1.
Sommers, P. (1984) *A guide to literature relevant to the organization and administration of nuclear power plants.* Washington, DC: Battelle Human Affairs Research Centers.
Stiglitz, J. E. (1979). A neoclassical analysis of the economics of natural resources. In V. K. Smith (Ed.), *Scarcity and growth reconsidered* (pp. 36-67). Baltimore, MD: Johns Hopkins University Press.
Stipp, D. (1990, August 30). Fluorescent-bulb sales become electrifying. *Wall Street Journal,* p. B1.
Sullivan, A. (1990a, September 17). Gasoline exports rise despite concern over supplies. *Wall Street Journal,* p. B1.
Sullivan, A. (1990b, August 17). It wouldn't be easy, but U.S. could ease reliance on Arab oil. *Wall Street Journal,* p. A1.
Sullivan, A. (1990c, July 30). OPEC may face long wait to see higher oil prices. *Wall Street Journal,* p. A4.
Synfuel baby is thrown out with the OPEC bathwater. (1981, March 13). *Economist,* pp. 182-194.
Tale, D. (1984, May 19). Senate ends deficit marathon, approves Reagan-backed bill. *Congressional Quarterly,* p. 1161.
Tanner, J. (1990a, April 6). Crude-oil prices register sharp drop on worries of possible glut in supply. *Wall Street Journal,* p. C6.
Tanner, J. (1990b, November 22). OPEC adds capacity, easing risk that cost of oil will soar in '90s. *Wall Street Journal,* p. A1.

Tanner, J. (1990c, October 5). Petroleum use starting to fall, agency reports. *Wall Street Journal,* p. A3.

Tanner, J. (1990d, September 6). Supplies of oil start to shrink, firming prices. *Wall Street Journal,* p. A3.

Tanner, J. (1990e, November 12). Surge in oil output could lead to a glut even if Persian Gulf standoff drags on. *Wall Street Journal,* p. A3.

Tanner, J., Murray, A., & Rosewicz, B. (1990, August 9). Crude-oil prices fall as Saudis and others plan to boost output to offset shortages. *Wall Street Journal,* p. A3.

Taylor, J., Nomani, A. Q., & Angrist, S. W. (1990, August 29). Hedgers enjoy an edge as oil prices swing. *Wall Street Journal,* p. B1.

Teece, D. J. (1983). Assessing OPEC's pricing policies. *California Management Review, 26,* 69-87.

Thomas, S. D. (1988). *The realities of nuclear power.* New York: Cambridge University Press.

Tsai, Hui-Liang (1989). *The energy illusion and economic stability: Quantum causality.* New York: Praeger.

Tugwell, S. (1988) *The energy crisis and American political economy.* Stanford, CA: Stanford University Press.

U.S. Congress, House Committee on Energy and Commerce. (1982). *U.S. Synthetic Fuels Corporation and national synfuels policy: Proceedings of a seminar by the Congressional Research Service.* (97th Congress, 2nd session). Washington, DC: Government Printing Office.

U.S. Congress, House Committee on Energy and Commerce. (1988). *Nuclear power plant standardization.* (House Hearing 100-206). Washington, DC: Government Printing Office.

U.S. Congress, House Committee on Energy and Commerce, Subcommittee on Energy and Power. (1987). *Alternative automotive fuels.* (House Hearing 100-87). Washington, DC: Government Printing Office.

U.S. Congress, House Committee on Energy and Commerce, Subcommittee on Energy and Power. (1989). *Advanced reactor technologies.* (House Hearing 101-17). Washington, DC: Government Printing Office.

U.S. Congress, House Committee on Interior and Insular Affairs, Subcommittee on Energy and the Environment. (1979, May 9-11, 15). *Accident at TMI, Oversight Hearings.* Washington, DC: Government Printing Office.

U.S. Congress, Senate Committee on Energy and Natural Resources. (1987a). *Domestic petroleum industry outlook.* (Senate Hearing 100-51). Washington, DC: U.S. Government Printing Office.

U.S. Congress, Senate Committee on Energy and Natural Resources. (1987b). *Greenhouse effect and global climate change.* (Senate Hearing 100-461). Washington, DC: Government Printing Office.

U.S. Congress, Senate Committee on Energy and Natural Resources. (1989). *DOE's national energy plan and global warming.* (Senate Hearing 101-235). Washington, DC: Government Printing Office.

U.S. Congress, Senate Committee on Energy and Natural Resources, Subcommittee on Energy Regulation and Conservation. (1989). *Automobile fuel efficiency standards.* (Senate Hearing 101-44). Washington, DC: Government Printing Office.

U.S. Congress, Senate Committee on Energy and Natural Resources, Subcommittee on Energy Research and Development. (1987a). *Conservation and solar energy research*

and development. (Senate Hearing 100-312). Washington, DC: Government Printing Office.
U.S. Congress, Senate Committee on Energy and Natural Resources, Subcommittee on Energy Research and Development. (1987b). *Renewable energy technologies.* (Senate Hearing 100-291). Washington, DC: Government Printing Office.
U.S. Congress, Senate Committee on Energy and Natural Resources, Subcommittee on Energy Research and Development. (1988). *Advanced reactor development program.* (Senate Hearing 100-846). Washington, DC: Government Printing Office.
U.S. Congress, Senate Committee on Energy and Natural Resources, Subcommittee on Energy Research and Development. (1989a). *Alternative motor vehicle fuels.* (Senate Hearing 101-141). Washington, DC:. Government Printing Office.
U.S. Congress, Senate Committee on Energy and Natural Resources, Subcommittee on Energy Research and Development. (1989b). *Energy efficiency and renewable energy research, development and demonstration.* (Senate Hearing 101-168). Washington, DC: Government Printing Office.
U.S. Congress, Senate Committee on Environment and Public Works, Subcommittee on Nuclear Regulation. (1980a). *Nuclear accident and recovery at Three Mile Island: A special investigation.* Washington, DC: Government Printing Office.
U.S. Congress, Senate Committee on Environment and Public Works, Subcommittee on Nuclear Regulation. (1980b). *Nuclear accident and recovery at Three Mile Island—A special investigation.* (Staff studies). Washington, DC: Government Printing Office.
U.S. General Accounting Office. (1980). *Three Mile Island: The most studied nuclear accident in history.* (EMD-80-109). Washington, DC: Author.
U.S. Nuclear Regulatory Commission. (1980a). *Action plan developed as a result of the TMI accident.* (NUREG-0660). Washington, DC: Author.
U.S. Nuclear Regulatory Commission. (1980b). *Clarification of TMI Action Plan Requirements.* (NUREG-0737).
U.S. Nuclear Regulatory Commission. (1982). *Human factors program plan.* (SECY-82-462).
U.S. Nuclear Regulatory Commission, Office of Inspection and Enforcement. (1979). *Investigation into the March 28, 1979, TMI accident.* (NUREG-0600).
U.S. Nuclear Regulatory Commission, Office of Nuclear Reactor Regulation. (1979). *TMI-2 lessons learned task force final report.* (NUREG-0585). Washington, DC: Author.
Vietor, R.H.K. (1984). *Energy policy in America since 1945: A study of business-government relations.* New York: Cambridge University Press.
Wald, M. L. (1990a, August 12). America is still demanding a full tank. *New York Times,* p. E3.
Wald, M. L. (1990b, September 6). Effect of fall in Soviet oil output. *New York Times,* p. D1.
Wang, Y., & Latham, W. (1989). Energy and state economic growth: Some new evidence. *Journal of Energy and Development, 14,*197-221.
Williams, R. H., & Larson, E. D. (1987). Materials, affluence, and industrial energy use. *Annual Review of Energy, 12,* 99-144.
Wood, W. C. (1983). *Nuclear safety: Risks and regulation.* Washington, DC: American Enterprise Institute.
Yu, U., & Choi, J. (1985). The causal relationship between energy and GNP: An international comparison. *Journal of Energy and Development, 10,* 249-272.
Zardkoohi, A. (1986). Competition in the production of electricity. In J. Moorhouse (Ed.), *Electric power* (pp. 63-97). San Francisco: Pacific Research Institute.

Index

About the Author

Alfred A. Marcus is Professor of Business, Government, and Society in the Carlson School of Management, the University of Minnesota. He formerly taught at the University of Pittsburgh Graduate School of Business and as an adjunct professor at the University of Washington Graduate School of Business. His Ph.D. is from Harvard (1977) in political science. He has an undergraduate degree in history from the University of Chicago and received a master's degree from the University of Chicago in political philosophy. From 1979 to 1984 he worked at the Battelle Human Affairs Research Centers in Seattle, where he was involved as an analyst in many of the energy policy issues that he describes in this book.

Other books by Professor Marcus include *Managing Environmental Issues* (with Rogene Buchholz and James Post) and *The Adversary Economy: Business Responses to Changing Government Requirements*. His articles have appeared in the *Academy of Management Journal,* the *Strategic Management Journal,* the *Journal of Policy History,* the *Journal of Law, Economics, and Organization,* the *Policy Studies Journal, Policy Sciences, Minerva,* and *Law and Policy.* His work on airline deregulation won the Theodore Lowi award as the outstanding article in the *Policy Studies Journal* in 1986. Professor Marcus has carried out research and done consulting for numerous government agencies and business organizations.